MINOR PROPHETS BIBLE STUDY

UNEARTH TIMELESS TEACHINGS OF THE
BIBLE'S UNSUNG PROPHETS

40-DAY BIBLE STUDY SERIES
BOOK 4

PETER DEHAAN

Minor Prophets Bible Study: Unearth Timeless Teachings of the Bible's Unsung Prophets

© 2020, 2022, 2025 by Peter DeHaan.

40-Day Bible Study Series, book 4

Library of Congress Control Number: 2025914835

Published by Rock Rooster Books

ISBN:

- 979-8-88809-023-7 (e-book)
- 979-8-88809-024-4 (paperback)
- 979-8-88809-025-1 (hardcover)
- 979-8-88809-026-8 (audiobook)

Credits:

- Developmental editor: Erin Brown
- Copyeditor: Robyn Mulder
- Cover design: Fanderclai Design
- Author photo: Chelsie Jensen Photography

CONTENTS

Who Are the Minor Prophets?   1

JONAH

Day 1: Jonah's Confession   9
Day 2: Worst Sermon Ever   12
Day 3: Self-Focused or Other-
Focused?   15
Dig Deeper: Prophets Pray   18

AMOS

Day 4: Fire and Destruction   23
Day 5: Chosen—and Disciplined   26
Day 6: Something God Hates   30
Day 7: The Lord Relents   34
Day 8: Israel Destroyed   37
Day 9: Israel Restored   40
Dig Deeper: The Kings of Judah   43

HOSEA

Day 10: Unfaithfulness   49
Day 11: Judgment or Mercy?   53
Day 12: What God Desires   57
Day 13: Foreign Words   61
Day 14: Spiritual Adultery and
Prostitution   64
Day 15: God Pursues Us, but Do We
Notice?   68

Dig Deeper: Idol Worship Then
and Now   71
Day 16: Walk with God and Do Not
Stumble   74

MICAH

Day 17: Stop It, Micah   79
Day 18: Godly Credentials   82
Day 19: What God Requires   85
Day 20: Our Hope   88
Dig Deeper: Spiritual Prostitution,
Unfaithfulness, and Love   91

NAHUM

Day 21: Our Refuge   97
Day 22: Doing God's Will May Not
Be Enough   100

ZEPHANIAH

Day 23: Complacency   105
Day 24: Lead Well   108

HABAKKUK

Day 25: How Long?   117
Day 26: Be Patient   120

OBADIAH

Day 27: The Sin of Inaction   125

HAGGAI

Day 28: Put God First   133
Dig Deeper: Be Strong   137

ZECHARIAH

Day 29: Returning   145
Dig Deeper: Astounding Parallels
between Zechariah and Revelation   149
Day 30: Wall of Fire   153
Day 31: If-Then   156
Day 32: Diligently Obey   160
Day 33: Better than Fasting   163
Day 34: Prophecy Fulfilled   166
Day 35: Shepherds and Sheep   170
Dig Deeper: Thirty Pieces of Silver   174
Day 36: Our Present and
Future Hope   177

JOEL

Day 37: A Holy Fast   183
Day 38: Swarms of Locusts   186

MALACHI

Day 39: Close Church?   191
Dig Deeper: Q & A with God   194
Day 40: God Challenges Us to
Test Him   197

The 40-Day Bible Study Series   201
For Small Groups, Sunday School, and
Classes   203
If You're New to the Bible   205
About Peter DeHaan   209
Books by Peter DeHaan   211

To Abigail

Series by Peter DeHaan

40-Day Bible Study Series takes a fresh and practical look into Scripture, book by book.

Bible Character Sketches Series celebrates people in Scripture, from the well-known to the obscure.

Holiday Celebration Devotional Series rejoices in the holidays with Jesus.

Visiting Churches Series takes an in-person look at church practices and traditions to inform and inspire today's followers of Jesus.

Be the first to hear about Peter's new books and receive updates at PeterDeHaan.com/updates.

WHO ARE THE MINOR PROPHETS?

A large portion of the Old Testament contains books of prophecy. Bible scholars divide these prophetic books into two categories. They call one group the Major Prophets, which includes the writings of Isaiah, Jeremiah (who also wrote Lamentations), Ezekiel, and Daniel.

The other category is the Minor Prophets, which we'll cover in this book. They are:

1. Hosea
2. Joel
3. Amos
4. Obadiah
5. Jonah

6. Micah

7. Nahum

8. Habakkuk

9. Zephaniah

10. Haggai

11. Zechariah

12. Malachi

This makes a total of twelve so-called Minor Prophets. The label *minor* is unfortunate because it leads many people to believe that their works and messages aren't as important as the Major Prophets. This isn't true. They're called minor because the books they wrote are shorter.

I, for one, like shorter books. It might be that you do too. The writings of these twelve prophets are quick to read and easier to digest.

We'll cover all twelve in *Dear Theophilus, Minor Prophets*. However, we won't address them in the order they appear in the Bible. Instead, we'll place them in chronological order (the best we can). This will give us some needed context and help us with continuity.

For many of these twelve prophets, the Bible lets us know the period of their ministries by mentioning the kings who ruled at that time, along with other useful hints. For other prophets, the Bible gives us no indication of when they prophesied. For these we place them in order based on Bible scholars' interpretations of nonbiblical historical documents. Several of the prophets in the following list have overlapping timelines, being contemporaries of one another and prophesying in the same era.

Here are the twelve Minor Prophets placed in rough chronological order. Key events and other notable biblical figures appear in parentheses to help us round out the timeline.

The nations of Israel and Judah in the Promised Land.

- **Jonah**
- **Amos**
- **Hosea**
- **Micah**
- (Isaiah, major prophet)

Assyria conquers Israel and deports many people. Only Judah remains.

- **Nahum**
- **Zephaniah**
- (Jeremiah, major prophet)

- **Habakkuk**
- **Obadiah**

Babylon conquers Judah and deports many people.

- (Daniel, major prophet)
- (Ezekiel, major prophet)

King Cyrus of Persia allows the people exiled from Judah to return and rebuild Jerusalem and the temple.

- **Haggai**
- (Zerubbabel, governor of Judah)
- (Ezra, priest and teacher)
- **Zechariah**
- (Esther, made queen by King Xerxes of Persia and Media)
- (Nehemiah, governor of Judah)
- **Joel**
- **Malachi**

With this timeline in mind, let's begin. It's sure to be an exciting journey.

If others give us an unfair label, like the Minor Prophets, how can we rise above it to best serve God?

[Discover more about another label in Judges 6:15 and the outcome in Judges 8:28.]

JONAH

Of the twelve prophets we'll cover, Jonah is the best known. He runs from God and spends a three-day time-out in the belly of a large fish. The Bible doesn't call it a whale—though it could have been one. It's simply a large fish.

Another notable fact about Jonah's book is that it is mostly a historical narrative and contains only the briefest of prophecies. Of all the prophets, Jonah is the least interested in sharing his message and the most successful.

Here is an overview of Jonah:

Known As: Jonah son of Amittai

Location: Gath Hepher (in Israel)

Occupation: prophet

Addresses: the people of Nineveh

Old Testament Mentions: 2 Kings 14:25

New Testament Mentions: Matthew 12:39–41, Matthew 16:4, and Luke 11:29–32

New Testament Quotations: none

Homonymous Mentions: One other man named Jonah is in Matthew 16:17.

DAY 1: JONAH'S CONFESSION
JONAH 1–2

He answered, "I am a Hebrew and I worship the Lord, the God of heaven, who made the sea and the dry land."

Jonah 1:9

The story of Jonah is familiar to many people. God tells Jonah to go to Nineveh and deliver a harsh message to the people there. Jonah doesn't. He ignores God, jumps on a boat, and heads in the opposite direction from Nineveh. He wants to get as far away as possible from what God wants him to do.

God brews up a storm, buffeting the ship carrying Jonah. The sailors do all they can to keep their boat afloat, including pleading for protection from their gods, while an oblivious Jonah sleeps through everything. When the storm grows fierce, they wake Jonah and confront him. He confesses. He admits he's running from God, the God he worships, the God who created both land and sea.

Now the sailors really freak out.

Though Jonah says the only solution is to toss him into the deep, as a living sacrifice of sorts to the sea, the sailors redouble their efforts, so they won't be guilty of their passenger's death. But eventually they give up, asking God not to hold them accountable for Jonah's murder. They throw him into the sea, and the waves calm. They are safe and presume Jonah is dead.

God has other plans.

A huge fish swallows Jonah. He spends three days lodged in the fish's belly. From there he prays. He calls upon God, and God listens. Jonah wraps up his prayer praising God and with another confession. He affirms that salvation comes from God.

Then God has the fish deposit Jonah on dry land. This isn't a smooth exit. It's a violent expulsion. The fish vomits and Jonah ejects.

There are similarities between Jonah and Jesus,

but we must take care not to carry the comparison too far—for it will lead us astray. Jonah offers himself as a sacrifice to save the lives of the men on the ship. As good as dead, he spends three days in the belly of the fish. Then he emerges from his effective tomb when the fish deposits him on dry land.

In much grander fashion, Jesus later offers himself as a sacrifice to save the lives of everyone. He dies so that we may live. After spending three days in his tomb, he rises from the dead, proving that he has mastery over death.

In a simple way, this part of Jonah's life foreshadows what Jesus will do for all humanity. Jonah at first ran from his responsibility, but Jesus never wavered. Thank you, Jesus.

Are we running from God as Jonah first did, or are we embracing God through what Jesus did?

[Discover more about Jesus's sacrifice in Matthew 12:40 and Mark 8:31.]

DAY 2: WORST SERMON EVER
JONAH 3

Jonah obeyed the word of the Lord and went to Nineveh.

Jonah 3:3

In underwater solitude, Jonah spends the next three nights and days inside the belly of a great fish. He has plenty of time to think about his situation. When the fish ejects him onto the shore, God speaks to Jonah a second time. "Go to Nineveh. And once you arrive, I will give you a message for the people."

This time Jonah obeys.

After what he endured for his first round of disobedience, I'm sure he doesn't want to encounter another incident of God trying to get his attention and offering correction. It seems less risky to say yes than to say no.

We don't know if Jonah repeats verbatim what God tells him to or if he paraphrases it a bit to fit his attitude. But what he says is both succinct and blunt. "In forty days Nineveh is going down."

This phrase stands as Jonah's only prophetic words in what reads like a book of history. As messages go, it neither convicts nor offers a hopeful alternative. He simply states as fact what will be, providing no instruction for the people to repent and realize a different outcome. We're left to wonder how much Jonah cares about the people he preaches to. Or if he even wants them to repent and turn their lives around.

In truth, Jonah surely longs to see their destruction. Here's why. Nineveh is the capital (or a principal city) of Assyria, a longtime antagonist of Israel and Judah. Surely Jonah and all his people would have cheered to see Assyria fall. They would view it as God's vindication for his chosen people, with him rescuing them from their adversaries.

It's no wonder Jonah doesn't put much effort into his message.

But the people of Nineveh believe that God will

do as Jonah says. They fast. They humble them-selves in the hope that God may relent and offer them compassion.

Guess what? He does. Forty days come and forty days go, with Nineveh avoiding the destruction God had planned.

How many times does God need to tell us something before we obey him? Do we obey with a good attitude?

[Discover more about God changing his mind in Exodus 32:9–14 and 1 Kings 21:29.]

DAY 3: SELF-FOCUSED OR OTHER-FOCUSED?

JONAH 4

"Isn't this what I said, Lord, when I was still at home? . . .
I knew that you are a gracious and compassionate God, slow
to anger and abounding in love, a God who relents from
sending calamity."

Jonah 4:2

First, Jonah disobeys God. Then, when he gets a second chance, Jonah obeys God but with a bad attitude. He gives the people of Nineveh a sorry little sermon that should have had no impact. But it does. In a shocking response, the people turn to God, and he spares them.

Jonah should be happy that the people repented. He should celebrate that God canceled the destruction of a large city. He should be delighted for the success of his words. But Jonah doesn't do these things. Instead, he's mad, angry. He vents his frustration to God in prayer. "This is why I didn't want to go in the first place," he complains. "I know you offer grace, compassion, and love. I knew from the start that you would give in and spare them."

Jonah may even be wondering what this unexpected outcome does to his credibility. He prophesied destruction, but destruction didn't happen. Will anyone believe him in the future should God give him another prophetic word to share?

Jonah has a pity party. He's ticked off. In a melodramatic overstatement, he tells God, "I've got nothing to live for. Just kill me now and get it over with." This is one prayer God doesn't answer.

Even though God has canceled his plans for the destruction of Nineveh, Jonah goes outside the city, finds a good vantage point, and sits down to see what will happen. God, in his sovereignty, provides unexpected shade for Jonah one day but removes it the next.

Jonah gripes about sitting in the hot sun. He vents his frustration. "Woe is me. I just want to die."

Jonah fixates on what people will think and the shade plant that died. He's so self-absorbed that he misses the reality that God used his words to save 120,000 people, along with many animals.

Jonah focused on his own comfort while God focused on the lives of others.

Do we seek our own comfort, or do we seek to save and rescue those around us?

[Discover a different attitude toward the lost in 1 Corinthians 9:19–23.]

DIG DEEPER: PROPHETS PRAY

"In my distress I called to the Lord, and he answered me."

Jonah 2:2

Though Jonah's experience is both interesting and unique, his ministry does not stand out as an example of what to do, but of what not to do. First he disobeys God. And when he finally halfheartedly warns Nineveh of their coming destruction, he's mad because they repent and avoid annihilation.

The book of Jonah records two of his prayers. In the first one, he calls out to God from inside the belly of the great fish. He's repentant of his actions and respectful to God. Jonah's second prayer stands as a bitter complaint against God and his mercy. Jonah's so dismayed—or so melodramatic—that he claims to prefer death over life.

Other prophets pray as well. Sometimes a fine line exists between a prayer, a psalm, and a prophecy. For example, Zechariah includes a passage that reads like a psalm, which includes brief prayers of phrase among prophetic proclamations.

Check out these prayers from our prophets:

- Joel 2:21–24
- Jonah 2:1–9
- Jonah 4:2–3
- Micah 7:14–20
- Habakkuk 1:2–4
- Habakkuk 1:12–2:1
- Habakkuk 3:2–19
- Zechariah 9:9–13

These prophets focus on prophesying, but they also record some of their prayers.

How can we better integrate prayer into our life and our work?

[Discover more about another prophet's powerful prayer in Daniel 9:4–19.]

AMOS

Following Jonah and slightly overlapping with Hosea we meet the prophet Amos. Occupationally he is a shepherd and does not identify as being a prophet.

Here is an overview of Amos:

Location: Tekoa, in Judah

Occupation: Shepherd

Addresses: many nations, primarily Israel

Kings: Uzziah (Judah) and Jeroboam (Israel)

Contemporaries: Hosea and Isaiah

New Testament Mentions: none

New Testament Quotations:

- Amos 5:25–27 in Acts 7:43
- Amos 9:11–12 in Acts 15:16–17

Homonymous Mentions: Another man named Amos appears in Luke 3:25.

DAY 4: FIRE AND DESTRUCTION
AMOS 1–2

They have rejected the law of the Lord and have not kept his decrees.

Amos 2:4

The book of Amos opens with a series of parallel prophecies about other nations. These form a pleasant rhythm. It goes like this: "For three sins, even four, I (God) will pour out my wrath. This is because [fill in the blank]. Therefore, I will send fire and consume your fortress, the thing you put your trust in."

In summary, they have sinned, and God will punish them.

Amos starts his series of prophetic punishments with Damascus. Then he moves to address Gaza, followed by Tyre, Amman, and Moab. How the people of Judah and Israel must celebrate these words of destruction against five of their enemies.

But then Amos follows the same pattern to warn the nation of Judah, which was once part of Israel. Together they comprise God's chosen people. Amos's prophetic warnings are getting close to home for the nation of Israel.

Judah's offenses are threefold. First, they rejected God's laws. Second, they failed to keep his decrees. Third, they followed false gods (lies). Though Judah is a nation of God's select, their punishment is the same as the first five nations. God will send fire, and it will consume their fortress, Jerusalem.

This should get the attention of the people of Israel. If they're honest with themselves, they will see that they too have committed the same three offenses as Judah, except they've done it more often and to a greater degree. They too have rejected God's laws, failed to keep his decrees, and followed false gods.

Yet I doubt they see this. I suspect they feel a

smug self-righteousness that God singled out Judah while sparing them his wrath. Not so fast.

Amos next launches into a tirade against Israel for their sins. He criticizes them for pursuing greed, oppressing the poor, and denying justice. Don't skip this list too fast. These sins remain a critical issue for us today.

Beyond that, they commit sexual depravity—a sin against one another. And they worship idols—a sin against God. Despite all he's done for them, they have not appreciated his protection or listened to his emissaries. Instead, the people force those who made vows to break them and tell God's prophets to keep their mouths shut.

At this point, Amos breaks from his pattern and does not proclaim that God will send fire to consume their fortress—yet.

When we read of God's criticism and correction in the Bible, do we apply it to others or to ourselves?

[Discover more about destruction by fire in Amos 5:6 and Revelation 20:14–15.]

DAY 5: CHOSEN—AND DISCIPLINED
AMOS 3–4

"You only have I chosen of all the families of the earth; therefore I will punish you for all your sins."

Amos 3:2

The Israelites (along with the nation of Judah) are God's chosen people. Here's how it starts. God calls Abraham to travel to a new place, where he will become a great nation and receive God's blessings. Abraham obeys. This establishes the foundation that will form the nation of Israel: Abraham is the father of Isaac, and Isaac is the father of Jacob. Jacob (aka Israel) is the father of twelve sons, whose descendants become the twelve tribes of Israel and later the nation of Israel.

Four centuries later, Moses emerges to lead Abraham's descendants from captivity in Egypt back to the land God promised to Abraham. God gives Moses rules for the people to follow and makes a pact with them, a covenant. He doesn't do this with any other nation. It's clear that God chooses them. They're his favorite people. The idea of God selecting them elevates them above all other people. This becomes so ingrained into Israel's conscious-ness that they divide all peoples accordingly. They are the Jews—the chosen—and the others are all Gentiles—not chosen.

Amos is one of the many writers of Scripture who confirm that God chose Abraham's descen-dants over all other nations and people. They're special. He likes them best. Having given them favored-nation status, it's logical that they would expect to live a VIP existence with no stress, trials, or opposition.

Though this could have happened—had they done a better job of following God and meeting his expectations—they will realize a different outcome: punishment for their errors.

Because God chose them, he singles them out

for punishment. He's not doing this to be cruel. God disciplines them because he loves them. He wants them to do better. He has pleaded with them for centuries through various judges and prophets who pointed them in the right direction.

Most of the time, however, the Israelites ignored God's ambassadors. And if the people did listen, they didn't adhere to his expectations for long. God will use another means to get their attention. It's time for the punishment phase.

Just as loving parents discipline their children, our loving Father in heaven disciplines us. Though this may seem like punishment at the time, it's corrective action to help us do better. It's pruning to prepare us to bear more fruit for him.

If God didn't love us so much and desire for us to be in right relationship with him, he wouldn't bother correcting us. He'd let us live whatever life we wished, not caring about the damage we cause or the consequences we suffer.

But just as God chose the Israelites to be his special people, he also chose to save us, and he loves us. Discipline, though not pleasant, is one way he shows his love.

Do we welcome God's correction as an act of love or resent him for causing us momentary pain?

[Discover more about God's discipline in Proverbs 3:11–12, Proverbs 19:20, Jeremiah 17:23, Amos 4:6, John 15:2, and Hebrews 12:4–11.]

DAY 6: SOMETHING GOD HATES
AMOS 5–6

*"I hate, I despise your religious festivals; your assemblies are
a stench to me."*

Amos 5:21

God is a God of love, but that doesn't
mean he loves everything. Some things
he hates. Quick, let's make a list. God
hates sin, evil, injustice, wickedness, sexual sin, idol
worship, wicked schemes, robbery, and wrongdoing.
He also hates double-mindedness, lies, murder, false
testimony, and rabble-rousing.

And there's one more thing God hates. It will
surprise you. He hates wrong worship.

Amos is blunt. God despises how his people celebrate their religious festivals. Their gatherings are a stench to him. Wait a minute. Aren't these things he told them to do? Yes. Through Moses, God commanded the people to hold several celebrations throughout the year. He told them to gather to worship him.

Did God change his mind? Does he want them to do something different now?

No, God hasn't changed his mind about the people gathering to celebrate him at their festivals. What he wants is for the people to change their attitude. He wants them to worship him in the right way.

Isaiah, a contemporary of Amos, later picks up the same theme. Isaiah gives more examples of the people's wrong worship. He tells them to stop bringing meaningless offerings to God, who says he detests the way they burn incense to him—even though he told them to do it. He labels their celebrations as worthless assemblies that he hates. What God prescribed as ways to draw his people to him, for them to connect, have become so perverted that it has the opposite effect. Their wrong worship drives a wedge between them and God.

Hosea, also a contemporary of Amos, addresses

PETER DEHAAN

this problem, albeit in a more positive way. Through Hosea, God says that it's more important for his people to offer others mercy instead of offering him sacrifices. God says he would rather have his people acknowledge him than give him burnt offerings. He doesn't want dead animals. He wants a living relationship with his people.

It's easy for us today to look back in time and shake our heads in dismay over the way God's people messed up their worship of him. Surely, we do better than that. Or do we?

What does God think of our worship today? I fear we have turned the relationship he desires into religious rules he hates. I worry that when we gather on Sunday, he despises what we do, that our going through rote rituals rises as a stench to him.

May this never be. May we learn to worship God in Spirit and in truth.

In what ways might our worship of God become something he hates? What must we change?

[Discover more about wrong worship in Isaiah

1:13–14 and what God wants in Hosea 6:6 and John 4:23–24.]

DAY 7: THE LORD RELENTS

AMOS 7

So the Lord relented. "This will not happen," the Lord said.

Amos 7:3

When Jonah preached destruction to the people of Nineveh, they turned to God and humbled themselves. God decided not to punish them and let them live. He changed his mind from what he intended to do based on the response of the people.

A similar thing happens with Amos, not once but twice.

God reveals to Amos what he plans to do. Amos

writes what the Lord *shows* him, but we don't know how God does this. It may be in a dream or through a vision. It could be that Amos is even in God's presence, seeing the preparations take place in a spiritual sense.

But then God reveals even more to his prophet. Amos witnesses God's planned destruction taking place. Swarms of locusts attack the crops just before harvest. They strip the land bare, leaving nothing to reap. Amos is aghast. "How will the people survive?" They'll starve.

Then God relents. He pledges that what Amos just saw will not occur. Or if it already happened, God undoes it. Nothing is beyond his power to accomplish.

But this isn't the end of the story. It merely concludes the first act.

God shows Amos something else. He calls for judgment by fire. (Recall what we covered in Chapter 4: "Fire and Destruction.") Fire dries up the water and devastates the land. Amos is even more shocked. He cries out to God. He affirms God's sovereignty to do whatever he wants to do while begging him to stop his destruction. "How will the people survive?" Amos asks again.

God relents. He pledges that what he just

showed Amos will not occur either. However, the story still isn't over.

For the third act, God shows Amos a plumb line —a tool used in construction to see if a building has proper alignment. God uses the plumb line in a spiritual sense to assess the character of his people. They fall short. "I won't spare them anymore," God says.

This time Amos doesn't protest. This time God doesn't relent.

Are we bold enough to ask God to change his mind? How many times will we do this?

[Discover more about another time when someone asked God to change his plans in Genesis 18:20–33.]

DAY 8: ISRAEL DESTROYED
AMOS 8:1–9:10

Then the Lord said to me, "The time is ripe for my people Israel; I will spare them no longer."

Amos 8:2

Next God shows Amos a basket filled with ripe fruit. "What do you see?" God asks.

Amos states the obvious, "A basket full of ripe fruit."

Then God shares his timing with Amos. "They are ripe. The people's time is up. I will delay their punishment no longer."

Again Amos remains silent. Though he protested God's first two plans of destruction, first by locust and then by fire, this time Amos says nothing. He remains silent. Just as he accepted God's assessment from the plumb line, Amos now accepts God's timing of when judgment will occur. How this must grieve the prophet, knowing that his words fell short to convict the people to turn their lives around and refocus on God, thereby receiving a stay to their sentence.

Though God says he will delay no longer—which we might understand to mean right away—remember that God views time differently than we do. A day to him is like a thousand years to us. But the opposite is also true. A thousand years to him is like a day to us. If this is perplexing, recall that at the formation of our world, God created spacetime. This means that he exists outside of time as we know it.

Regardless of when God's judgment will occur, it will be horrific. Temple songs will turn into funeral wails. Bodies, countless bodies, strewn everywhere. And then dead silence.

The sun will set at noon. Festivals will become funerals, with songs morphing into weeping. The people left will mourn those who died, a bitterness too great to comprehend. Famine will follow, but not a physical one, a divine one instead. In this spiritual famine the people will be unable to hear what God has to say.

They'll stagger. They'll wander. And they'll search for a word from God. But they'll find nothing. No one will escape. All sinners will die.

We can view this prophecy as having already occurred or still to happen or both.

How does this prophecy impact how we live and what we do today?

[Discover more about God's view of time in Psalm 90:4 and 2 Peter 3:8, as well as Mark 13:32 and 1 Thessalonians 5:1–2.]

DAY 9: ISRAEL RESTORED

AMOS 9:11–15

"I will plant Israel in their own land, never again to be uprooted from the land I have given them," says the Lord your God.

Amos 9:15

Though the destruction of Israel seems like the end, it's not. There's more. After the punishment of destruction comes restoration. Amos wraps up his otherwise dismal prophecy with a passage of hope.

Amos writes that in that day, God will rebuild Jerusalem, repair its walls, and restore what their enemy ruined. Food will be plentiful, and wine will flow with abundance. People will return from their exile. They will rebuild. They will live in the land that was once theirs. They will sow and harvest and eat.

God will replant Israel—his people—in their own land. This is permanent. Never again will he uproot them and send them away. This is the land he has given them, and it is theirs forever. This is what God says. It will happen.

This prophecy of restitution can have multiple interpretations in God's amazing timeline. In the near term, the people hauled off to captivity will experience repatriation. This happened about five centuries before Jesus came to earth, and it represents the first fulfillment of Amos's prophecy of restoration.

For the mid-term, we see the return of Israel as a nation. This happened in 1948. We can also see this as the fulfillment of Amos's prophecy of restoration.

For the long-term, in a future we wait to see, we can envision a coming restoration. We will witness a new heaven and a new earth. In this future resting place, we'll forget our past pains. Right living will prevail. Jesus will spiritually marry his church, and we'll live with him forever. This stands as the final fulfillment of Amos's prophecy of restitution.

With two restorations complete, the ultimate restoration awaits. What a glorious day that will be.

Are you ready? Are you excited?

How does our future restoration reflect in how we live, act, and talk today?

[Discover more about the new heaven and the new earth in Isaiah 65:17, Isaiah 66:22, 2 Peter 3:13, and Revelation 21:1.]

DIG DEEPER: THE KINGS OF JUDAH

*"The Lord God will give him the throne of his father David,
and he will reign over Jacob's descendants forever; his
kingdom will never end."*

Luke 1:32–33

Many of the prophets served during the reigns of certain kings of Judah. Here is a list of the kings of Judah, all descendants of King David through his son King Solomon—along with the prophets who ministered during their rule.

- Rehoboam

- Abijah
- Asa
- Jehoshaphat
- Jehoram
- Ahaziah
- Joash
- Amaziah (possibly Jonah)
- Azariah/Uzziah (possibly Jonah and Amos)
- Jotham (Hosea and Micah)
- Ahaz (Hosea and Micah)
- Hezekiah (Hosea and Micah)
- Manasseh (possibly Nahum)
- Amon
- Josiah (Zephaniah)
- Jehoiakim (possibly Habakkuk)
- Jehoiachin (possibly Habakkuk and Obadiah)
- Zedekiah (possibly Habakkuk and Obadiah)

The prophets Haggai, Zechariah, Joel, and Malachi all prophesy *after* the fall of the nation of Judah, so there are no kings, even though the line of David continues—to Jesus and through Jesus.

We will not find our names written in the Bible

along with these kings and prophets, but our names can appear in God's book of life.

Is your name written in God's book of life? Through Jesus, it can be.

[Discover more about King David's descendants in 1 Chronicles 3:10–16 and Matthew 1:6–17. Read about God's book of life in Philippians 4:3, Revelation 3:5, and Revelation 20:15.]

HOSEA

Coming alongside and following Amos is Hosea. God tells Hosea to marry a prostitute and then use their relationship as an object lesson for the people. It's a poignant lesson in unfaithfulness, disappointment, and unconditional love.

Here is an overview of Hosea:

Known As: Hosea son of Beeri

Addresses: Israel and Judah

Kings: Uzziah, Jotham, Ahaz, and Hezekiah of Judah and Jeroboam of Israel

Contemporaries: Amos, Micah, and Isaiah

New Testament Mentions: Romans 9:25

New Testament Quotations:

- Hosea 1:10 in Romans 9:26
- Hosea 2:23 in Romans 9:25
- Hosea 6:6 in Matthew 9:13 and Matthew 12:7
- Hosea 10:8 in Luke 23:30 and Revelation 6:16
- Hosea 11:1 in Matthew 2:15
- Hosea 13:14 in 1 Corinthians 15:55

Homonymous Mentions: There are no other men in the Bible named Hosea.

DAY 10: UNFAITHFULNESS
HOSEA 1–2

The Lord said to him, "Go, marry a promiscuous woman
and have children with her, for like an adulterous wife this
land is guilty of unfaithfulness to the Lord."

Hosea 1:2

God calls Hosea to be his prophet and tells him to marry a prostitute. This is one of God's most shocking directives.

It's intriguing that God doesn't tell Hosea which prostitute to marry. Hosea gets to choose. While he can opt for the first one he sees, pick one at random, or select the woman most needy or deserving of rescue, I suspect he does none of these.

Remember, Hosea is a guy. I imagine he picks the most alluring prostitute. This makes the story even more scandalous.

Now, picture young Hosea coming home and telling his parents: "Guess what? God came to me and told me that I'm going to be his spokesman." His parents beam with pride. Then he drops a bombshell. "And God told me to marry a prostitute."

This seems so inappropriate, so ill-advised, so . . . ungodly. Yet that is what God says to do. And Hosea obeys.

The strangeness doesn't stop there. Each time his wife, Gomer, gets pregnant, God tells Hosea to give the kids some curious names.

First, she bears him a son, whom God says to call Jezreel. The name is to prophetically pronounce punishment on Israel, which will occur in the Jezreel Valley.

Next, Gomer gives birth to a girl, who receives a name that means "not loved." Then a second son receives a name that means "not my people." The girl's name suggests that Hosea might wonder if he's the father, while the son's name implies that he isn't. How this must pain God's prophet—and Hosea's kids.

Later, Hosea's wayward wife splits, returning to her former life. But the story doesn't end there. God tells Hosea to search for her and take her back. Hosea finds her, but he must buy her freedom. He must redeem her. We can assume this is either because she's racked up some debts, or he needs to buy her out of the sex industry.

What a horrific ordeal for Hosea.

Let's recap. God tells him to marry a prostitute. Hosea chooses Gomer. She produces three children, two of whom probably aren't his. Then Gomer runs away and returns to prostitution. God tells Hosea to go find her, even though she's undeserving. He does, but he must pay to get her back.

This is all part of God's plan so that Hosea can use Gomer's infidelity as a series of sermon illustrations to the people of Israel about their unfaithfulness to God. This includes prostituting themselves with other gods, figuratively producing offspring through their adultery, and then running away from God. Still, he wants them back. He searches for them, finds them, and pays for their return.

This is a profound object lesson for us too. Regardless of what we do, how badly we mess up, or how far we stray, God loves us unconditionally and pursues us relentlessly.

Do we fully realize and adequately appreciate just how much God loves us?

[Discover more about Gomer in Hosea 3:1–3, and read some of Hosea's related prophecy in Hosea 2:2–23.]

DAY 11: JUDGMENT OR MERCY?
HOSEA 3–4

"I will not punish your daughters when they turn to prostitution, nor your daughters-in-law when they commit adultery, because the men themselves consort with harlots."

Hosea 4:14

As Hosea continues his rant against spiritual prostitution and adultery, his words seem to morph into a double meaning, implying both a spiritual and a physical application.

God says that he won't punish the people's daughters when they turn to prostitution. Nor will he discipline their daughters-in-law when they commit adultery. The reason? They don't engage in these acts alone. The men participate too, taking a lead role.

In a spiritual sense, this implies that the person who leads someone else into spiritual adultery deserves greater punishment. But the person who follows them into it will go unpunished.

Now let's look at the physical aspect. We start with the Law of Moses. He writes that when a man commits adultery with another man's wife, both the man and the woman must die. A common form of execution in that day is stoning.

Fast-forward to Jesus in the New Testament. The Pharisees have this rule from Moses in mind when they bring a woman caught in the act of adultery to Jesus. They ask what he thinks about Moses's command that she must die by stoning. Though their query seems legitimate, they're trying to trap Jesus. They want to maneuver him into saying something they can use against him.

Jesus sees through their ruse. He doesn't answer their question directly. Instead, he gives permission to anyone who is without sin to pick up the first rock and hurl it at the adulterous woman. Since no one is sinless, one by one they all slink away in humiliation. In this way, Jesus offers the woman mercy as opposed to judgment.

This also serves as a reminder not to judge others for their sins because we have sinned too.

However, there's another element to this story. Where's the guy? It takes two to commit adultery, right? Why did the Pharisees only haul in the woman and not drag the man before Jesus? It's because they have a double standard. It may even be that one of their own was the adulterous man. In their minds, the woman deserves death, but the man's involvement isn't worth noting.

In economic terms, there needs to be both supply and demand for a market to exist. This applies to prostitution and adultery. Society and the church tend to focus on the *supply* side of the fornication equation. God's focus seems to be on the *demand* side.

From both the spiritual and physical perspective, the person who initiates should receive punishment. At the same time, the other person, though not guiltless, receives mercy.

PETER DEHAAN

How does this unexpected passage in Hosea inform how we should respond to sexual sin, specifically prostitution and adultery?

[Discover more about what the Bible says about prostitution and adultery in Leviticus 20:10, Proverbs 6:26–29, and John 8:3–11.]

DAY 12: WHAT GOD DESIRES
HOSEA 5–6

"For I desire mercy, not sacrifice, and acknowledgment of God rather than burnt offerings."

Hosea 6:6

The first five books of the Bible talk a lot about God's expectations of his people. He gives Moses his laws to guide them in right behavior, both what they're supposed to do and what they're to avoid. The Bible also discusses —sometimes in excruciating detail—the complex array of sacrifices and burnt offerings God expects his people to regularly give him. Many of these occur according to the calendar, while others relate to life events. It seems the people are never far away from an occasion to worship God through offering a sacrifice.

Because of the repeated emphasis on sacrifices in the Old Testament, it's easy to conclude they're the focal point of worshiping God. Or are they?

Hosea casts into doubt this assumption regarding the importance of animal sacrifices. He does this when he shares God's perspective on this involved practice—which, incidentally, seems both wasteful and barbaric to most people today.

What God says through Hosea is that he wants his people to offer mercy and not sacrifices. He wants them to acknowledge him rather than present him with slaughtered animals.

Though it may be an overstretch to say that God wants them to stop offering animal sacrifices, he certainly is calling for a change in perspective. Could it be that the people's hearts are not in the right place when they offer their sacrifices? They might be going through the motions of a ritualistic religious practice while having lost all connection to the reason behind the rite—and the God who instituted it.

So it is when we blindly follow traditions that evolved over time without a thought or care to the original goal of the practice.

If God doesn't want dead animals anymore, consider what he wants instead. He asks that his people be merciful to others. Giving mercy—and not insisting on judgment—emerges as a form of worship, one which God desires. Think about it. We honor God by how we treat others and not some religious ritual that has ceased to hold meaning for us.

Next, God says that he wants his followers to acknowledge him. The original intent of the burnt offerings was to point to him, acknowledging him as Lord. But if the burnt offerings now fail to do that, it makes sense to eliminate them and encourage the people to focus directly on him.

When we offer mercy to others, we honor God by reaching out to other people. When we acknowledge God as Lord, we honor him by reaching up to him.

How do we honor God? What forms of worship have become meaningless rituals for us that we must change?

[Discover more about honoring God in Psalm 46:10, Luke 12:8, John 4:24, and 1 John 4:15.]

DAY 13: FOREIGN WORDS
HOSEA 7–8

"I wrote for them the many things of my law, but they regarded them as something foreign."

Hosea 8:12

In this passage, Hosea again quotes God. God says that he gave his people detailed instructions—that is, his law—but he laments that they don't understand or follow his words.

If you've spent much time reading God's laws in the Old Testament, specifically those in the books of Leviticus and Deuteronomy, I suspect you comprehend the people's confusion. Some of the contents of these books seem quite foreign to us today and are hard to comprehend. Our eyes blur over the details. We become tempted to skim or even skip the passages altogether.

The people in Hosea's time don't have God's Word in printed form. Producing a copy of Scripture was a time-consuming endeavor and costly undertaking since scribes handwrote copies on manmade scrolls. This means that most people don't have the opportunity to study God's law. Instead, they must listen as priests read it to them or teach them about it, assuming the religious leaders bother to do so. No wonder the law God wrote to his people seems foreign even to them.

Things are much different today. In most parts of the world, we have access to his Word. It's printed in inexpensive and easy-to-produce books. And it's readily available online in multiple versions.

One roadblock to accessing God's Word is in countries where possessing a Bible is a crime. The other barrier is for people who don't yet have the Bible translated into their native language. For the rest of us, being able to read and study the Bible is a realistic option. And we should pursue it with diligence.

Yet many people today regard God's words in the Bible as foreign. In large part, this is because

they haven't bothered to read it. Another consideration is that they may rely on what other people tell
them about the Bible, which may be in error.
Having wrong information is a definite cause for
confusion.

Granted, some passages of the Bible are confus-
ing. Over the centuries, biblical scholars have
debated what these verses mean, so it's okay if a few
passages seem foreign. But if most of the Bible
seems foreign to us, it's a sign that we may need to
spend time reading and studying its words.

*Do the words of the Bible seem foreign? Why? What should
we do about it?*

[Discover more about studying the Bible in Psalm
119:11, Acts 17:11, and 2 Timothy 3:16.]

DAY 14: SPIRITUAL ADULTERY AND PROSTITUTION

HOSEA 9–10

For you have been unfaithful to your God; you love the wages of a prostitute at every threshing floor.

Hosea 9:1

A recurring theme in Hosea's prophecy is unfaithfulness. Instituted by God's command, Hosea tragically suffers because of his wayward wife's unfaithfulness. This example of physical unfaithfulness symbolically points to the nation's spiritual unfaithfulness to God. God uses Hosea's heartbreaking relationship as a distressing object lesson to get his people's attention.

As Hosea endures the agony of his life and attempts to communicate God's message to his people, he also uses two scandalous words that relate to this idea of unfaithfulness: *adultery* and *prostitution*. If the term *unfaithfulness* doesn't cause them —and us—to squirm, surely mentioning adultery and prostitution will.

Just as Hosea's wife, the former prostitute, cheats on him by committing adultery, the nation of Israel commits spiritual adultery against God. His chosen people are unfaithful to him, prostituting themselves with false gods to satisfy their divine desires apart from God. They commit spiritual adultery by pursuing spiritual intimacy with other gods.

God is not pleased.

Today few people commit this type of unfaithfulness by physically bowing in reverence and worship before a manufactured idol. We would never commit adultery with that type of god. We would never spiritually prostitute ourselves in this way.

Yet we are unfaithful to God. We cheat on him. We commit spiritual adultery. We spiritually prostitute ourselves. It's just that our wayward pursuits take on quite a different form today than how the Israelites were unfaithful to God in Hosea's time.

Many people today are busy, too busy. We try to squeeze in as much activity as we can into the twenty-four hours God gives us each day. We practice time management and overschedule ourselves and our families. And as we do so, we push God aside, forgotten. Our full schedules take precedence over him.

Another persistent prostitution in today's world is our pursuit of accumulating wealth, be it money or possessions. We've lost sight of the fact that we need money to live. Instead, we live for money. Earning money, spending money, and accumulating money can become an all-encompassing priority. Our focus on money distracts us from God. In doing so, we're unfaithful to him.

A third consideration for much of today's society is pleasure and comfort. People go to great lengths to avoid unpleasantness or stress. We pursue things to make us feel good, things that distract us from the reality of life. These diversions can take on many forms, but two things about them are true. One, these "gods" provide only a short-term escape. And second, these pursuits push God aside and take over his rightful place.

These are just some of the ways we can be unfaithful to God today. We commit spiritual idolatry and even prostitute ourselves to these worldly pursuits, which sideline our Lord.

Fortunately, God is patient. He offers grace and mercy. He waits for us to return to him and leave unfaithfulness behind. The next move is ours.

How might we be unfaithful to God? What do we need to do to fully return to him?

[Discover more about what Hosea says about spiritual prostitution in Hosea 4:10–18, Hosea 5:3–4, and Hosea 6:10.]

DAY 15: GOD PURSUES US, BUT DO WE NOTICE?
HOSEA 11–12

"But the more they were called, the more they went away from me. They sacrificed to the Baals and they burned incense to images . . . they did not realize it was I who healed them."

Hosea 11:2–3

As the prophet Hosea winds down his writings, he gives us insight into the heart of God. He writes that the more God called his people, the more they ran away from him.

Imagine God beckoning us, longing for us to be in a relationship with him. With much expectation he calls our names. His invitation is gentle, sweet, welcoming. But instead of hearing his call and running into his warm embrace, we turn our backs on him and dash in the opposite direction. It's as if he offers us a high five or a fist bump, but we leave him there, hanging, poised to receive a response we will never offer.

How this must grieve him.

We've all had this happen to us. We extend ourselves to others: to family, neighbors, friends, and church. But instead of receiving the response we hope for, the reaction we long for, we hear only silence or even a sharp rebuff. How their rejection grieves us. How it tears at our souls.

Now multiply this by thousands, by millions, by billions. That's how many of humanity's numbers snub God's call and ignore his persistent love. It breaks my heart, and more surely it breaks his—a billion times over.

Yet God responds not in anger but in love. He still cares for his people, just as he cares for us now. He still wants the best for them, and he wants the best for us.

And what's more, though he heals them, they do not realize it comes from him. They do not attribute their good outcomes to his loving care. What about us? Do we recognize when God heals us? Healing can address many aspects of our being: spiritual, physical, and emotional. If we're not seeing his healing in our lives, it may be because we're not looking hard enough.

When God calls us, may we answer him. When he heals us, may we thank him.

How does God call us and heal us? How will we respond?

[Discover more about God calling us in 1 Corinthians 1:9, 2 Thessalonians 2:14, 1 Peter 1:15–16, and 1 Peter 2:9–10. Read what else Hosea says about God healing us in Hosea 6:1.]

DIG DEEPER: IDOL WORSHIP THEN AND NOW

"Do not make any idols."

Exodus 34:17

The prophets in the Bible talk a lot about not worshiping idols, that is, deifying manmade images, objects, and ideas instead of revering God. Most of our twelve Minor Prophets condemn this practice, with Hosea leading the way. Amos, Jonah, Micah, Nahum, Habakkuk, Zephaniah, and Zechariah also denounce idol worship. (Other prophets who rail against idols are Isaiah, Jeremiah, and Ezekiel.)

Many of them point out the folly of this practice. Men make an image out of wood or precious metals. They ascribe irrational importance to their creations and worship them as though they possess intellect and ability. In truth, these idols are inert. They can't do or accomplish anything.

From the perspective of our world today, we see the utter foolishness of worshiping idols. We would never do something so idiotic. Or would we?

In truth, we have our idols today too. It's just that our idols are seldom figures we make. Our idols today are activities and pursuits we chase after, placing more importance on them than chasing after God.

What might these idols be?

For many it is money, power, or prestige. It could be the ability to influence others or receive their respect. We can also put careers, friends, and family ahead of God. Even a hobby or a passion can become our idol, replacing God as the most important priority in our life.

None of these quests are necessarily bad, though we must keep them in their rightful place. But when their importance to us supersedes our relationship with our Lord, who created us and the world we live in, we risk setting up these pursuits as idols that we worship.

What things in our lives threaten to push God aside? What must we do to realign our priorities?

[Discover more about the folly of worshiping idols in Hosea 13:2, Amos 5:26, and Habakkuk 2:18, as well as Isaiah 40:19–20, Isaiah 44:12, Jeremiah 10:14, and Ezekiel 16:17.]

DAY 16: WALK WITH GOD AND DO NOT STUMBLE

HOSEA 13–14

The ways of the Lord are right; the righteous walk in them,
but the rebellious stumble in them.

Hosea 14:9

As Hosea concludes his prophecy with this final section, he urges Israel to turn away from their shortcomings and return to God. When they do, blessings will follow, blessings for them and blessings for others through them. Once again, we have this concept in the Bible of God blessing his people so that they can, in turn, be a blessing to others.

After these words from God, Hosea tacks on a

final thought. He confirms that God's ways are right. Those who are righteous walk with God. They follow him. But those who rebel against God will stumble.

If we find ourselves tripping over what God tells us to do, this could imply we're being rebellious. But this doesn't mean we can't ask questions. I suspect God enjoys our questions—if we're sincere in finding truth and ask with right motives. But if we disregard what he says, we shouldn't be surprised when we fall.

Some people read the Bible and delight in it. They're happy to follow God and walk in his ways.

Other people read the Bible and mock it. They think it's outdated. Yet in ignoring the truths it contains they trip over it. Then they ask, "Why don't things work out for me?" "Why is my life such a mess?" or "Why can't I catch a break?" But this is what happens when we rebel against God and don't do what he tells us.

Though God doesn't force himself on anyone, a person can't rebel against him and ignore his words and then expect to receive his blessings. People who disregard what God says will trip and fall. Ironically, these rebellious people then often blame

God for their troubles. But he didn't cause them. They did.

We can't have it both ways. We can't ignore God and expect him to bless us anyway.

Walk with God, and do not stumble over what he says to do.

How can we better walk with God? When bad things happen to us, whom do we blame?

[Discover more about walking with God in Genesis 5:21–24, Genesis 6:8–9, Deuteronomy 8:6, Galatians 5:16, and 1 John 2:6.]

MICAH

The prophet Micah is a contemporary of Isaiah. Micah's ministry overlaps and follows Hosea's. We know little about Micah from the Bible.

Here is an overview of Micah:

Known As: Micah of Moresheth

Addresses: Israel and Judah

Kings: Jotham, Ahaz, and Hezekiah of Judah

Contemporaries: Hosea and Isaiah

Old Testament Mentions: Jeremiah 26:18

New Testament Mentions: none

New Testament Quotations:

- Micah 5:2, 4 in Matthew 2:6
- Micah 7:6 in Matthew 10:35–36

Homonymous Mentions: The Bible includes five other men named Micah. Most notable is Micah in the book of Judges (Judges 17–18).

DAY 17: STOP IT, MICAH
MICAH 1–2

"Do not prophesy," their prophets say. "Do not prophesy about these things; disgrace will not overtake us."

Micah 2:6

The prophet Micah delivers strong words from God to his people. Although his proclamation (prophecy) should convict them, it doesn't. Instead, they take offense. At one point, the other prophets—false prophets—tell Micah to stop talking, as if his silence will keep God's plans from happening.

Micah's sarcastic retort is that if a prophet proclaims plenty of wine and beer for everyone, the people will flock to him. Rather than face truth, the people prefer to anesthetize themselves from it.

But telling the people what they want to hear—as opposed to the truth—is making a false prophecy. Regarding these false prophets, Micah further notes that when the people feed them (or pay them), the prophets say positive things. They pronounce that peace will occur. And if they don't say what the people want to hear, the people turn against them.

Our reaction to things we don't want to hear is much the same today.

When we read a passage in the Bible we don't like, one that offends us, what do we do? The first reaction of many is to breeze past it and pretend we never read it. This effectively cuts the passage from Scripture, turning the Holy Bible into a Bible with holes. Other people look for clever ways to try to ascribe a different meaning to that verse, making it say something it doesn't.

What about when a preacher or teacher says something that offends us? We can opt to let those words convict us, change us, and reform us. Or we can dismiss that person and their words, moving on to find someone else who will speak only comforting thoughts and pleasant platitudes.

When we do this, we become consumers,

leaving the teacher of an unpalatable message and seeking someone who will tell us what we want to hear. This is a consumerist mindset: looking for what is pleasant and nice—even if it's wrong.

It happened to Micah, to Isaiah, and even to Jesus. And it's still happening today.

How do we react when we read something in the Bible we don't like? How do we respond when a preacher offends us by telling us what the Bible says, even if it's politically incorrect?

[Discover more in Isaiah 30:10–11, Micah 3:5, Matthew 13:57, Mark 6:2–5, and John 6:60–66.]

DAY 18: GODLY CREDENTIALS
MICAH 3–4

But as for me, I am filled with power, with the Spirit of the Lord, and with justice and might.

Micah 3:8

As Micah continues to write and prophesy, he shares his credentials. It's not the type of resumé most people today would celebrate. He doesn't brag about where he went to school or the degrees he earned. He doesn't talk about the size of his church, growth rates, or the number of years in ministry. Nor does he say how many people he speaks to regularly, the accuracy of his prophecies, or the number of his conversions. Though these are the things many people esteem, they don't matter to Micah. And I suspect they don't matter to God.

Micah says that he's filled with power, God's spirit, justice, and might.

First is power. Some versions of the Bible couple power with the second item on the list, the Holy Spirit, as in Holy Spirit power. Yet most versions separate these two traits. Another word for power might be *strength*. This isn't physical but spiritual. It's supernatural vigor, even courage. It exhibits itself in character traits such as self-control, ability, and authority.

Next, Micah possesses the infilling of the Spirit of the Lord, the Holy Spirit. This means he has God's guidance, influence, and perspective directing what he does and the things he says.

Third is justice, a recurring theme in Old Testament prophecies. It's also a character trait that we would do well to reclaim today. It means doing what is right and being fair in all things to all people.

Micah's final characteristic is might. It seems closely aligned with the first one, power. But in the text, it's coupled with justice. The suggestion is justice administered with might. Again, this is not a physical force but more so a spiritual intensity.

Micah applies these four traits to himself, claiming them as his credentials for doing God's work. But as with many passages in the Bible's prophetic books, we can see a double meaning.

We are right to apply these four characteristics to Jesus too. He moved in power, possessed the Spirit of the Lord, promoted justice, and acted with great might. Though no New Testament verse makes this connection, we see Jesus's life fulfilling Micah's prophecy.

Now let's take this one step further and apply it to ourselves. We would do well to claim these as our own credentials for ministry and service. And if we can't claim them, let's pursue them.

In what credentials do we place our confidence?

[Discover more about these four godly credentials in Matthew 12:18, Luke 4:18, 2 Corinthians 3:17, 2 Corinthians 7:11, Ephesians 1:18–20, and Colossians 1:11.]

DAY 19: WHAT GOD REQUIRES
MICAH 5–6

And what does the Lord require of you? To act justly and to love mercy and to walk humbly with your God.

Micah 6:8

Micah slips a profound thought into his writing. In one concise sentence, he states what God requires of his people. It's succinct and simple. It's startling but weighty. Equally astonishing is what Micah doesn't include in his list of things God requires.

God doesn't say go to church, develop the right theology, or obey a bunch of rules. Yet these are some of the many things we put great importance on today. We focus on these elements—and others like them—at the expense of what God requires.

What does God require from us?

First, God wants us to act justly. We often hear the word *justice*, but we don't often hear of acting justly. What does acting justly mean? Here are some ideas: we should be honorable and fair in how we deal with others, behave morally (that is, be righteous), and do all things properly.

Does this sound like Jesus? It's what he taught and how he acted. Yet we often forget to behave this way ourselves. Instead, we become sidetracked chasing secondary pursuits and even focusing on goals that don't matter in God's perspective.

Next, God requires that we love mercy. This goes beyond merely showing mercy to others but to fully embracing it. Many times people show mercy but do so begrudgingly. Their attitude is wrong. Though they show mercy, they don't love it. In fact, they may hate it. God wants us to love showing mercy to others. Isn't that what he does for us? Shouldn't we follow his example and do it for others?

Last, God requires that we walk humbly with him. Humility is a word we don't hear much anymore. In today's culture, humility is no longer an esteemed characteristic. In truth, most people look down on the humble and dismiss them. Instead, society embraces the bold, egotistical, and controversial. However, in God's kingdom, this is the wrong perspective. God requires us to walk humbly with him. And when we walk humbly with him, the natural outgrowth is humility toward others.

Though Micah directs these expectations of God's requirements to the nation of Israel, these points align with God's character and are more broadly applicable to us.

Yes, these fall short of a command for us to obey today. But if God expected his people to do this thousands of years ago, is there any reason we should ignore it today?

We are to pursue justice, embrace mercy, and walk with God in humility.

How willing are we to apply these three requirements of God to ourselves?

[Discover more about God's requirements in 1 Kings 2:3.]

DAY 20: OUR HOPE
MICAH 7

But as for me, I watch in hope for the Lord, I wait for God my Savior.

Micah 7:7

As Micah wraps up his prophecy to the people of Israel, he laments about what he sees around him. All the godly and righteous people are gone. Those who remain kill and do evil. The leaders are corrupt, demanding gifts and accepting bribes. People distrust one another and dishonor those in their family. This is a sad state for God's chosen people.

But then Micah slips into first person and shares

his perspective. It's quite a contrast. Unlike those around him, he says he will *watch* and *wait* hopefully for God, who will save him. Micah uses these two verbs to show us what he's doing.

First, Micah watches in hopeful anticipation for God to show up. Micah is on the lookout, expectant for what God will do. Like a sentry, he keeps watch. He is attentive. This is an example of diligence. Even though everyone else has turned their backs on God, Micah hasn't. He's willing to stand alone, placing his hope in the Lord, in what he has promised, and in what he will do.

Though there are times in the Bible when God tells us to watch for him, there are also instances of God watching us. He watches over us and protects us in all that we do. How comforting to know that God watches over us. As a result, we are right in watching for him in expectation.

The second action is to wait. Micah waits for God to come and rescue him. This is a lesson in patience. Patience may be a virtue we embrace, but it's a practice we have trouble living out. In today's world, we are increasingly impatient people. We want things now, not later. We aren't willing to wait, sometimes not even a few seconds. But Micah is content to wait patiently for God.

And God is content to wait patiently for us. He wants to give us every chance to turn to him.

Do we watch in hope for God? Do we patiently wait for him to act?

[Discover more about waiting for the Lord in Psalm 27:14, Psalm 130:5–6, and Isaiah 8:17. Learn more about watching in Habakkuk 1:5 and Luke 12:37.]

DIG DEEPER: SPIRITUAL PROSTITUTION, UNFAITHFULNESS, AND LOVE

"All her idols will be broken to pieces; all her temple gifts will be burned with fire; I will destroy all her images. Since she gathered her gifts from the wages of prostitutes, as the wages of prostitutes they will again be used."

Micah 1:7

The prophets in the Bible often condemn the people for their prostitution. Sometimes this refers to the physical act and other times it's spiritual. Often the first is an allusion to the second. Hosea, Joel, Amos, Micah, and Nahum all address this uncomfortable topic, as do three of the major prophets: Isaiah, Jeremiah, and especially Ezekiel, who leads all others, mentioning prostitution twenty-eight times.

When the Bible addresses spiritual prostitution, it refers to the people's unfaithfulness to God. They cheat on him with other gods. They cheat on him with idols. And they cheat on him by turning away and ignoring him and his commands.

Being unfaithful to a spiritual being is abstract. It's intangible and difficult to comprehend. It's easy to downplay its significance because it doesn't seem real. Spiritual unfaithfulness is a concept, so it's easy to dismiss. Spiritual prostitution is conceptual, making it hard to grasp.

It becomes more real, however, when prostitution is physical, tangible. Recall Chapter 14: "Spiritual Adultery and Prostitution" about Hosea and his unfaithful, prostitute of a wife. She cheats on him. She runs away. But Hosea pursues her. He buys her back, takes her home, and offers her a love she doesn't deserve.

This is how God treats us when we're unfaithful to him. He pursues us, buys us back, and takes us home. He offers us unconditional love, even though we don't deserve it.

How might we be unfaithful to God today? Are we ready to accept his forgiveness and unconditional love?

[Discover more about God's immense love for us in Psalm 36:5–7, Psalm 52:8, Psalm 136, Romans 8:38–39, and Ephesians 3:18–19.]

NAHUM

Following closely after Micah (and Isaiah) is Nahum, who appears only once in the Bible. Therefore, we know nothing about him from Scripture, though we do know that, like Jonah, he prophesies destruction against the city of Nineveh and the nation of Assyria. This time the people of Nineveh do not repent.

Here is an overview of Nahum:

Known As: Nahum the Elkoshite

Location: Nahum is an Elkoshite, but that name doesn't appear elsewhere in the Bible, so it gives us no hint about Nahum's heritage or where he is from.

Addresses: the city of Nineveh (in the nation of Assyria)

New Testament Mentions: none

New Testament Quotations: none

Homonymous Mentions: One other Nahum appears in the Bible. He is from Jesus's family tree (Luke 3:25).

DAY 21: OUR REFUGE
NAHUM 1

The Lord is good, a refuge in times of trouble. He cares for those who trust in him.

Nahum 1:7

A refuge is a place of protection from danger or difficulty. We all need a safe place at one time or another. Our sanctuary may be from physical danger, spiritual attack, or emotional assault. It may be a shelter we occasionally retreat to or a haven where we regularly reside.

When we need protection from whatever presses in around us, where do we go to be safe?

Too often we attempt to make our own retreats. They may be our homes, our money, or our possessions. But if we depend on these things for our security, they will eventually let us down. Material comforts may console us for a time, but trusting in our belongings to save us will disappoint us in the end.

Another option is to seek people as our refuge. This may be family or friends. It could be church, an aid organization, or government resources. While each of these options can help for a time, especially family and friends, these solutions have limitations.

Other times we retreat to places to ensure our safety. These may be a physical fortress or an emotional stronghold, but they can do only so much. Some people may seek sanctuary in a church building. This may be for physical protection or for spiritual solace. Though church is a noble retreat, it too has limits.

The Bible shows us a better way. God can be our refuge. We can retreat to him when trouble approaches, when life overwhelms, or when the salvo of the enemy becomes too much to bear.

Nahum confirms that we can turn to God, the good Lord, for our refuge when trouble threatens.

He will care for us in our times of need. All we need to do is place our trust in him.

Does this mean that seeking refuge in God is conditional on us trusting him? Nahum isn't clear on this, but why wouldn't we want to place our full reliance on God? We can trust him to save us from physical, emotional, and spiritual attacks, both now and forever.

We can trust God to be our refuge during troubled times.

Is God truly our sanctuary? What does he shelter us from?

[Discover what other prophets say about refuge in Isaiah 57:13, Jeremiah 16:19, Joel 3:16, and Zephaniah 3:7.]

DAY 22: DOING GOD'S WILL MAY NOT BE ENOUGH
NAHUM 2–3

"I am against you," declares the Lord Almighty.

Nahum 2:13

Nahum's prophecy is against Nineveh. As a major city, likely the capital of Assyria, God's verdict against Nineveh is representative of his sentence against the whole country.

Does the city of Nineveh sound familiar? I hope so. It's the city that the reluctant Jonah went to. His assignment was to preach God's message of judgment and destruction. But the people listened to Jonah's words. They took his message seriously. In hope that God might change his mind, they turned to him and sought him.

Much to Jonah's dismay, God relented and did not destroy the city. At least not then.

About one century later, Nahum comes onto the scene. He also prophesies the destruction of Nineveh and, implicitly, Assyria along with it. At this time Assyria has already conquered Israel and deported many of its people. This happened between Jonah's visit to Nineveh and Nahum's prophecy against it.

Had God not changed his mind when Jonah declared Nineveh's destruction, they would not have been around to later attack and overthrow Israel. Think about it. God spared Nineveh (Assyria), and they later conquered Israel, God's chosen people.

God used Assyria to punish Israel for their repeated disobedience and unfaithfulness. This doesn't mean God favored Assyria, merely that the nation was his tool to accomplish what he had warned his people would happen.

Though some may think God unfair to punish Assyria for accomplishing his purpose, that's exactly what he will do. Nahum makes this clear when he writes God's declaration that he opposes Nineveh.

Just because Assyria fulfilled God's will doesn't

mean it found favor with him or that he will spare the nation from punishment for the evil it did. Is it too much of a stretch to consider that we could do God's will but still fall short of his expectations and therefore receive punishment?

Again, this may seem unfair, but when we accomplish God's sovereign will, it isn't a means to secure our salvation. We can't earn eternity through our behavior. We realize our salvation when we follow Jesus and believe in him to save us.

Do we think that doing God's will should save us? In what ways are we basing our eternal status on the things we do?

[Discover more about salvation in Matthew 10:38–39, Luke 14:27, John 8:12, Acts 16:31, and Romans 10:9.]

ZEPHANIAH

Following Nahum is Zephaniah. The only information the Bible gives us about Zephaniah is his parentage and that he prophesies during the reign of King Josiah. Zephaniah is the son of Cushi, grandson of Gedaliah, great-grandson of Amariah, and great-great-grandson of Hezekiah.

Here is an overview of Zephaniah:

Known As: Zephaniah son of Cushi

Addresses: many nations, including Judah and exiled Israel, along with everyone (the whole world)

King: Josiah of Judah

New Testament Mentions: none

New Testament Quotations: none

Homonymous Mentions: Three other men in the Bible are named Zephaniah, though none are well-known.

DAY 23: COMPLACENCY
ZEPHANIAH 1

"At that time I will search Jerusalem with lamps and punish those who are complacent, who are like wine left on its dregs, who think, 'The Lord will do nothing, either good or bad.'"

Zephaniah 1:12

Z ephaniah has critical words for the people who live in Jerusalem and, by implication, all of God's people. They live smug, self-satisfied lives. This is because they assume God is distant. They don't believe he will act. And they're quick to say so. They dismiss the Lord, claiming he won't do a thing, neither good nor bad to them—nothing positive and nothing negative. He won't reward them, and he won't punish them. He is aloof —or so they claim—leaving them free to live unexamined, complacent lives.

Complacent means to be "pleased or satisfied" or especially to be "extremely self-satisfied." The city of Jerusalem harbors people who have a smug self-satisfaction for their lives.

This describes many people I know.

Though not materially satisfied, they're spiritually satiated. They're content to sit back with no concern for their spiritual well-being and little remorse for a lifestyle that falls far short of what it could be, of what it should be, and of what God desires. In a word, they're content. They have a smug self-satisfaction that they do more good than bad. This is okay for them. They're spiritually satisfied, which makes them spiritually dead.

God doesn't like complacency. Through the prophet Zephaniah, he says he will search out these smug people and punish them. They're even unworried about his threats to their complacency, for they assume he will do nothing to them, neither good nor bad. They're self-satisfied with their relationship to God, and he is angry.

Another group of people who suffer from smug self-righteousness is the church in the city of

Laodicea. Jesus's disciple John writes about them in his epic vision we call Revelation, the last book of the Bible. To the people of Laodicea, God simply says he will spit them out, for they are complacent: neither hot nor cold. He can do nothing with them, so he will spew them from his mouth. What an apt image of disgust. And for anyone who wants to be close to God, what a frightening picture of separation.

May God never find us complacent. The consequences are too great.

What must we do to guard against spiritual complacency?

[Discover more about complacency in Revelation 3:15–17.]

DAY 24: LEAD WELL
ZEPHANIAH 3

Her prophets are unprincipled; they are treacherous people.
Her priests profane the sanctuary and do violence to the law.

Zephaniah 3:4

After proclaiming judgment on the entire earth and specifically picking on the complacent people in Jerusalem, Zephaniah goes on to prophesy against many other nations. This includes Philistia (Gaza, Ashkelon, Ashdod, and Ekron), Kerethite, Canaan, Moab, Ammon, Kush, and Assyria. How the people of Israel must love Zephaniah's railing against their enemies, about his prophesying their doom.

Then Zephaniah gets personal. He directs his rant to Jerusalem. After talking about the people in general, he focuses his attention on their leaders. He addresses their officials, rulers, prophets, and priests.

These last two categories—prophets and priests—represent the people's spiritual leadership. About the prophets, Zephaniah says they are unprincipled and treacherous. About the priests, that they profane the worship of God.

We want our spiritual leaders to guide us well and point our focus to Jesus. Yet these prophets fall far short. Lacking principles, their ethical downfall causes them to act with a profit motive, not a spiritual perspective. As a result, their actions deceive the people, doing harm and not producing good. To them, God doesn't matter. What motivates them is the money they can earn through their positions. They don't serve the Lord or his people. They serve themselves and their unquenchable desire for wealth and power.

Likewise, these priests fall short too. They desecrate God's holy sanctuary of worship by promoting idolatry. In doing so, they bring what is contrary to God into the very place intended to worship only him. They also likely offer blemished animals as sacrifices, contrary to the law. How these things disrespect God.

We, of course, would never do this today. Would we?

After first addressing our own motivations and actions, we must scrutinize our spiritual leaders and hold them accountable to a higher standard. While most do their jobs admirably, a few fall short, damaging the good news of Jesus and the reputation of his Father.

What motivates and drives these supposedly godly people? Let's look at two general areas.

The first is money. Do our spiritual leaders live lavish lifestyles? Do they live a life of luxury, far better than those they serve? This hints that something might be out of balance. Even more convicting are those who promote giving at the expense of talking about Jesus. They harp more about their listeners' need to give money to the "ministry" than the people's need to have Jesus in their lives. I've heard these preachers. I suspect you have too.

The second major category is worship. Do our spiritual leaders promote worship practices not found in the Bible? While not all deviations are bad in themselves, some are dangerous. Far worse, do they advocate worship practices contrary to what Scripture says?

These are all warnings to watch out for in our leadership—and in our own lives.

How can we make sure our worship best aligns with God's desires? How can we encourage our spiritual leaders to lead us well and with integrity?

[Discover more about the importance of leadership in Matthew 18:6, Acts 20:28, 1 Timothy 3:7, Titus 2:7–8, and James 3:1.]

HABAKKUK

Following Zephaniah by a few years is Habakkuk. His ministry overlaps Jeremiah's and most of Obadiah's. He prophesies just before Judah's fall to Babylon. Unlike the other prophets' writings, Habakkuk's book records a dialogue between him and God, with God's response emerging as prophecy. Habakkuk concludes with a lengthy prayer that reads like a psalm.

Here is an overview of Habakkuk:

Location: likely Judah

Occupation: prophet

Addresses: the people of Judah

Kings: the Bible doesn't say, though it could have been during the reigns of Jehoiakim, Jehoiachin, and Zedekiah

Contemporaries: Jeremiah and Obadiah

New Testament Mentions: none

New Testament Quotations:

- Habakkuk 1:5 in Acts 13:41
- Habakkuk 2:3 in Hebrews 10:37
- Habakkuk 2:4 in Romans 1:17, Galatians 3:11, and Hebrews 10:38

Homonymous Mentions: There are no other men in the Bible named Habakkuk.

DAY 25: HOW LONG?

HABAKKUK 1

How long, Lord, must I call for help, but you do not listen?

Habakkuk 1:2

W hen we seek God, he always responds immediately, right? When we pray, he answers fast, doesn't he? And when we're in a jam and ask for help, he's always quick to rescue us, correct?

Yes, sometimes God reacts right away when we need him. But other times we wait—and wait. We're left to wonder, "How long?"

Habakkuk understands this delay. He, too, asks God, "How long?" Though Habakkuk calls for help

—and has been calling for help—the Lord God doesn't respond. It's as if God isn't listening to Habakkuk's laments.

As Habakkuk cries out to God for rescue, the prophet continues to observe ongoing injustice all around him. God's lack of response suggests he tolerates the wrong living and wrong actions of his people. Habakkuk feels surrounded by destruction and violence, hemmed in by strife and conflict. The law means nothing. Injustice prevails. Evil abounds.

How long? How long must he wait?

Habakkuk isn't the first person to ask this question. This simple two-word query pops up often throughout the Bible. As you might suspect, it's most common in the Psalms, the Bible's book of prayers—a prayer journal, if you will. In these prayers of David and others, the question *how long?* occurs fifteen times.

Jeremiah asks this question eight times, leading all prophets. Along with Jeremiah and Habakkuk, four other prophets ask God the same thing: Isaiah, Daniel, Hosea, and Zechariah.

But sometimes when the Bible poses this question, it's not us asking God, "How long?" It's God asking us. How long will we refuse to obey him and follow his commands? How long will we treat our

Lord with contempt by dismissing him? How long will we refuse to believe in Jesus, despite all he's done for us? And Elijah, acting as God's spokesman, asks the people how long they will continue to waiver between two perspectives: God or Baal.

Though we don't struggle with worshiping Baal today, we face temptations to worship many other things rather than God. How long will we vacillate between God and a counterfeit?

How long will we wait for God to answer the angst of our souls? And how long will we make God wait for us?

[Discover more about us asking God "How long?" in Psalm 6:3, Psalm 119:84, and Jeremiah 12:4. Read about God asking us "How long?" in Exodus 16:28, Numbers 14:11, 1 Kings 18:21, and Proverbs 1:22.]

DAY 26: BE PATIENT
HABAKKUK 2–3

For the revelation awaits an appointed time; it speaks of the end and will not prove false. Though it linger, wait for it; it will certainly come and will not delay.

Habakkuk 2:3

After Habakkuk asks God his pointed question "How long?" before the prophecy finds fulfillment, God answers —sort of. Yes, it would be nice for God to say that the time is right, and he will respond now. Or he could give a definite time, such as in six months or within this decade. Even answering, "During your lifetime" would help.

But these aren't the types of answers God gives. Instead, he says he has already appointed the time for the prophecy's fulfillment. Therefore, Habakkuk must wait. From his viewpoint it delays and lingers, but the prophecy will most certainly occur as promised. Habakkuk must stand by. He must have confidence that God's prophecy is true and will happen just as he said it will, when the time is right.

Habakkuk must be patient. We covered patience in Chapter 20: "Our Hope." There Micah says that he will watch and wait for the Lord. He will watch expectantly, and he will wait in anticipation for God to show up and do what he will do.

This same theme of perseverance comes up again here in Habakkuk. God tells Habakkuk to eagerly wait. The Lord has already decided when the prophecy will find its fulfillment. Though from Habakkuk's perspective, God is slow to act, it will happen.

Patience applies to us too. Whether we're anticipating the fulfillment of one of the Bible's prophecies or expecting an answer to prayer, we must endure. We must abide with God-honoring restraint, knowing that he will come through for us when the timing is right. Yes, we must be patient with God.

God is also patient with us, slow to become angry when we fail him. He wants us to have every opportunity to repent, return to him, and follow him.

But beyond our waiting with patience for God and him being patient with us, he also calls us to do the same in our dealings with others. And this may be even harder to do than waiting on God.

How patient are we with God? How patient are we with others?

[Discover more about patience in Job 6:11, Ephesians 4:2, 1 Thessalonians 5:14, and 2 Peter 3:9.]

OBADIAH

Overlapping Habakkuk and following him is Obadiah. His one-chapter book in the Bible records what God reveals to him in a vision.

Here is an overview of Obadiah:

Location: likely Judah

Addresses: Edom, the descendants of Esau

King: the Bible doesn't say, though it could have been during the reigns of Jehoiachin and Zedekiah

Contemporaries: Habakkuk

New Testament Mentions: none

New Testament Quotations: none

Homonymous Mentions: The Bible has eight other men named Obadiah, though none are noteworthy.

DAY 27: THE SIN OF INACTION
OBADIAH 1

"On the day you stood aloof while strangers carried off his wealth and foreigners entered his gates and cast lots for Jerusalem, you were like one of them."

Obadiah 1:11

O badiah speaks against the nation of Edom. Among other things, he criticizes Edom for its pride. The primary issue, however, is not what the people of Edom did but what they didn't do. Theirs is not an act of commission, but of omission. Their sin is inaction.

The gripe God has against them is for the violence afflicted on the nation of Judah. Not that

Edom committed the violence themselves, but that they stood by and watched as other nations did, failing to come to Judah's aid.

For this error, God has destined that they will wear their shame as a covering, which all will see. Further, God promises to destroy their nation forever. They won't receive punishment for a season. Instead, they're receiving a life sentence with no chance of parole. The nation of Edom will end. This is a harsh judgment for doing nothing. God offers no forgiveness to Edom and no chance for restoration. He announces only punishment.

This shows us God's heart. He wants us to act justly, and we see his displeasure with those who stand idly by and don't help those in trouble.

We are guilty of this today. Consider the evils that pervade our world. List the injustices that confine too many people. Catalog the crises we have become immune to. Here's a list to start our thinking: war, genocide, ethnic cleansing, famine, lack of clean drinking water, mass incarceration, violence, religious persecution, unfair laws and unequal enforcement, corrupt judges and government officials, and on and on it goes. I'm sure you can add more.

The list is long. It's also overwhelming. These

cruelties grieve God's heart. And they should grieve ours too. While it's not feasible for us to personally address every one of these issues, we can do our part to help some of them, or at least one of them.

As a starting point, the Bible often talks about the importance of meeting the needs of the poor, orphans, widows, and foreigners. This is a great place to start. When we see someone in need, exploited, or receiving unfair treatment, may we act and not stand aloof like Edom.

How must we change our views about people needing help? Where can we make a difference in the lives of others and our world?

[Discover more about helping others in Exodus 22:22, Deuteronomy 14:28–29, Isaiah 1:17, Jeremiah 7:6–7, Malachi 3:5, and James 1:27.]

HAGGAI

Haggai is the first prophet to emerge after the people of Judah return from their exile in Babylon. He challenges them to rebuild the temple, noting that God's house lies in ruins while the people have built fine houses for themselves. Ezra remarks that the people prosper under the preaching of Haggai, a fine tribute to his effectiveness as God's messenger.

Here is an overview of Haggai:

Location: Judah

Occupation: prophet and preacher

Addresses: the exiles who have returned to Judah from Babylon

King: Darius of Persia

Contemporaries: Zechariah, Zerubbabel, and Ezra

Old Testament Mentions: Ezra 5:1 and Ezra 6:14

New Testament Mentions: none

New Testament Quotations: Haggai 2:6 in Hebrews 12:26

Homonymous Mentions: There are no other men in the Bible named Haggai.

DAY 28: PUT GOD FIRST
HAGGAI 1–2

"You expected much, but see, it turned out to be little. What you brought home, I blew away. Why?" declares the Lord Almighty. "Because of my house, which remains a ruin, while each of you is busy with your own house."

Haggai 1:9

I n his short, two-chapter book, Haggai has a message for the people as well as an application for us today. God, through Haggai, chastises his people. They live in nice homes while God's home—the temple—sits in shambles.

God has been trying to get his people's attention

for years, but they miss it. Now he tells them to look at their situation. He reels off a list of realities:

- Each year you plant much but harvest little.
- You eat but are never full.
- You drink but are still thirsty.
- You put on clothes but remain cold.
- You earn money, but it doesn't last until your next paycheck.

God tells them to contemplate these facts. He wants his people to put him first and think about their own needs second. When they do this, he will give them plenty.

In this specific case, God wants them to rebuild his temple, reestablishing it as their center of worship. Though we could assume this means he wants us to embark on a building project for our churches—making it our number one priority—this misses the modern-day application. Remember, Jesus came to fulfill the Old Testament, so the need for a physical temple ended because—through Jesus —we are his temple.

God wants his people to put him first and think

about their own needs second. When they do this, he will meet their needs. Today, we can receive this Old Testament prophecy as a call to put Jesus first. This is an easy enough lesson.

However, it gets a bit dicey when we dig into this. Based on the lesson from Haggai, we could assume that if things aren't going our way and we aren't receiving God's blessings, it's because our priorities are out of whack, and we aren't putting him first in all that we do. Though sometimes this may be the case, other times we may struggle and suffer because God is growing us into the people he wants us to become. In this case, we may have our priorities correct and, for a season, still not enjoy his blessing.

If we feel we aren't receiving God's blessings, it's up to us to determine why. Do we need to reorder our priorities, or do we need to allow him to grow himself in us, preparing us for the future?

May we wisely discern the reason why.

What are our priorities? Do we truly put Jesus first?

[Discover more about putting God first in Exodus 20:3, Proverbs 3:5–6, Matthew 6:33, Matthew 22:37–40, John 15:5, and Revelation 2:4.]

DIG DEEPER: BE STRONG

"Be strong, all you people of the land," declares the Lord,
"and work. For I am with you," declares the Lord Almighty.

Haggai 2:4

Throughout the Bible we see the phrase *be strong*. Sometimes this is a command and other times it's encouragement. Both Haggai and Zechariah include the phrase *be strong* in their prophecies.

For Haggai, the situation is prior to the rebuilding of the temple by the remnant who returned to Judah. At God's instruction, Haggai tells Zerubbabel, the governor who leads the project, to *be strong*. Then Haggai tells Jozadak, the high priest, to *be strong*. The people will need strong leadership to complete this important work of reconstructing God's temple.

Not only do the leaders need strength but the people also need strength. After encouraging Zerubbabel and Jozadak to *be strong* leaders, Haggai tells all the people to *be strong* too. Everyone will need strength—both physical and emotional—to complete the reconstruction of God's temple.

In his prophecy, Zechariah, a contemporary of Haggai, also includes the instruction for the people to *be strong* so that they may rebuild the temple. And a bit later, he encourages the people by promising that God will save them, and they'll become a blessing to others. Therefore, "Don't be afraid. Be strong."

Two Major Prophets, Isaiah and Ezekiel, like- wise tell the people to *be strong*. But we first encounter the encouragement to *be strong* in Deuteronomy. Here the phrase is "be strong and courageous." Moses tells this to the people before they are about to enter Jericho and conquer the land God promised for them, the land where

Abraham first settled. Moses encourages the people to "be strong and courageous." Then he repeats the charge to Joshua, who will succeed him in leadership.

After Moses's death, God speaks to Joshua and tells him the same thing, "Be strong and courageous." Paul may have these passages in mind when he writes to the believers in the city of Corinth to be courageous and strong, as a general instruction for right living.

Throughout the Bible, God encourages his people to *be strong* so they can complete the work before them. He tells this to Moses, Joshua, and the people before they retake the Promised Land. He tells it to Zerubbabel, Jozadak, and the people before they rebuild his temple. And it isn't hard to imagine him telling us today to "be strong and courageous" as we pursue the assignments he gives us.

What is God asking us to do? How can we go in strength to do what God is telling us to do?

[Discover more about the prophets telling the people to "be strong" in Isaiah 35:4, Zechariah 8:9, and Zechariah 8:13. Read about being strong and courageous in Deuteronomy 31:6–7, Joshua 1:6–9, and 1 Corinthians 16:13.]

ZECHARIAH

The fourteen-chapter book of Zechariah is the longest of all the Minor Prophets. Though the book of Zechariah has more chapters than Daniel, whom scholars classify as a Major Prophet, Daniel has more content and is therefore a longer book.

Here is an overview of Zechariah:

Known As: Zechariah, son of Berekiah

Location: Judah

Occupation: prophet and shepherd

Addresses: the exiles who have returned to Judah from Babylon

King: Darius of Persia

Contemporaries: Haggai, Zerubbabel, and Ezra

Old Testament Mentions: Ezra 5:1 and Ezra 6:14

New Testament Mentions: Matthew 23:35

New Testament Quotations:

- Zechariah 4:3, 11, 14 in Revelation 11:4
- Zechariah 9:9 in Matthew 21:5 and John 12:15
- Zechariah 11:12–13 in Matthew 27:10

- Zechariah 12:10 in John 19:37 and Revelation 1:7
- Zechariah 13:7 in Matthew 26:31 and Mark 14:27

Homonymous Mentions: We find many men in the Bible named Zechariah, perhaps more than any other name. With the number of obscure mentions of Zechariah throughout the Bible—fifty-nine times in nine books—it's impossible to accurately list how many there are, but there are perhaps twenty-two. The main ones are Zechariah, king of Israel; Zechariah, the prophet, whom we cover here; and Zechariah, father of John the Baptist.

DAY 29: RETURNING
ZECHARIAH 1

"Therefore tell the people: This is what the Lord Almighty says: 'Return to me,' declares the Lord Almighty, 'and I will return to you.'"

Zechariah 1:3

Zechariah begins his prophecy with God calling his people to return to him. This is nothing new. It seems that much of the Old Testament is God telling the Hebrew people to come back to him. Accompanying these calls comes a threat of punishment or a withholding of blessings if they don't respond.

This time it's different.

This time God's call for the people to return carries a promise that he will return to them when they do. It seems both parties have pulled away from each other. An intentional separation occurred, as if each turned their back on the other. The people turned from God, and then he turned from them.

This reminds me of Jesus on the cross. In the middle of his turmoil, a despair greater than we could ever comprehend, Jesus cries out to his Father, "Where are you? Why have you abandoned me?"

Since God is too pure to gaze at evil, and because Jesus, at that moment, carries the accumulated weight of everyone's sins for all time, Father God must look away. It's as if God momentarily turns his back on Jesus. He must endure the agony of his sacrifice for us alone, without his Father's support. Thank you, Jesus!

Fortunately, their separation is brief. They return to each other, never again to separate.

Consider Jesus's parable of the prodigal son (better called the two sons). This allegory is about a father and his two boys. The older son is compliant while the younger son is rebellious. The younger boy has the audacity to ask his father for his share of the inheritance while Dad is still alive.

The father agrees. The son grabs the money and takes off. He turns his back on his dad. The young man squanders his inheritance on an undisciplined, rowdy lifestyle. Soon his money is gone. Penniless, starving, and in despair, he recalls how well his father treats his hired hands. They have it much better than the son does. The young man returns home in humility. He'll beg the father he disrespected to hire him as a laborer. Then he'll have enough to eat.

Watching for his boy to return, the father spots him at a distance. He runs out and embraces his son. Dad reinstates the boy into the family. To celebrate, the father throws a lavish party. He explains his rationale to the older son. "Your brother once was dead but is alive again. He once was lost but is now found."

So it is whenever anyone returns to God. He'll reinstate them as his heir and throw a lavish celebration. They were dead but are now alive. They were lost but are now found.

God doesn't want any of us to perish. If we disrespect him and turn our backs on him, he's

PETER DEHAAN

waiting, looking for us to return. When we do, he'll throw a party.

Is God calling us to return to him? Do we believe he'll take us back?

[Discover more about Jesus's sacrificial death for us in Psalm 22:1, Habakkuk 1:13, and Mark 15:34. Read about Jesus's parable of the two sons in Luke 15:11–32.]

DIG DEEPER: ASTOUNDING PARALLELS BETWEEN ZECHARIAH AND REVELATION

"During the night I had a vision."

Zechariah 1:8

The book of Zechariah and the book of Revelation, which contains John's grand vision, have over two dozen parallel images that occur as the prophets look toward the future. The similarities are so striking that we stand in amazement as we consider them.

- Red horse in Zechariah 1:8; 6:2 and in Revelation 6:4; 9:17

- White horse in Zechariah 1:8; 6:6 and in Revelation 6:2; 19:11
- Peace on earth in Zechariah 1:11; 9:10 and in Revelation 1:4
- Zion in Zechariah 1:14; 1:17; 2:7; 2:10; 8:2–3; 9:9; 9:13 and in Revelation 14:1
- Four horns in Zechariah 1:18 and in Revelation 9:13
- Measure in Zechariah 2:2 and in Revelation 11:1–2; 21:15–17
- Four winds in Zechariah 2:6 and in Revelation 7:1
- Seven eyes in Zechariah 3:9; 4:10 and in Revelation 5:6
- Inscription/inscribe/written in Zechariah 3:9; 14:20 and in Revelation 1:3; 2:17; 13:8; 14:1; 17:5; 17:8; 19:12; 19:16; 20:15; 21:12; 21:27; 22:7
- Stone in Zechariah 3:9 and in Revelation 2:17; 17:4; 18:12; 21:19
- Bowl in Zechariah 4:2–3; 9:15; 14:20 and in Revelation 5:8; 15:7; 16:1–4, 8, 10, 12, 17; 17:1; 21:9
- Two olive trees in Zechariah 4:3, 11 and in Revelation 11:4

- Gold lampstand in Zechariah 4:2 and in Revelation 1:12–13; 1:20; 2:1
- Mountain in Zechariah 4:7; 6:1; 14:4–5 and in Revelation 6:14–16; 8:8; 16:20; 21:10
- Temple in Zechariah 4:9; 6:12–15; 8:9; 9:8 and in Revelation 3:12; 7:15; 11:1; 11:19; 14:15; 14:17; 15:6; 15:8; 16:1; 16:17; 21:22
- Foundation in Zechariah 4:9; 8:9; 12:1 and in Revelation 21:14, 19
- Scroll in Zechariah 5:1–2 and in Revelation 1:11; 5:1–9; 6:14; 10:1–2; 10:8–10; 22:7, 9–10, 18–19
- Chariots in Zechariah 6:1; 9:10 and in Revelation 9:9
- Black horse in Zechariah 6:2; 6:6 and in Revelation 6:5
- Dappled horse/pale horse in Zechariah 6:6 and in Revelation 6:8
- Spirits in Zechariah 6:5 and in Revelation 1:4; 3:1; 4:5; 5:6; 16:13–14
- Jerusalem in Zechariah (40 mentions) and in Revelation 3:12; 21:2; 21:10
- Holy Mountain in Zechariah 8:3; 14:5 and in Revelation 21:10

- Eyes in Zechariah 9:1; 14:12 and in Revelation 1:14; 2:18; 3:18; 4:6, 8; 5:6; 7:17; 19:12; 21:4
- Earthquake in Zechariah 14:5 and in Revelation 6:12; 8:5; 11:13; 11:19; 16:18

Are we amazed when we read God's Word? Are we excited for the future he has prepared for us?

[Discover more about the future in Joel 2:28–32.]

DAY 30: WALL OF FIRE
ZECHARIAH 2

"And I myself will be a wall of fire around it," declares the Lord, "and I will be its glory within."

Zechariah 2:5

One night the prophet Zechariah has a vision. In this supernatural dream, he talks to an angel who is about to measure the city of Jerusalem to see just how big it has become. But before he leaves to do this, another angel arrives. He tells the first angel that it doesn't matter. There are now so many people in Jerusalem that erecting walls around them to keep them safe

PETER DEHAAN

isn't an option. The city is too big, and building a wall isn't feasible.

Living in an unwalled city would normally leave the residents vulnerable to attack and abuse from their enemies. But now there's no need for concern. In this case, the Lord God will himself become the city's wall. He will protect his people. He'll do this by becoming a wall of fire around the city. And then his glory will shine from within.

What a powerful image.

There is now no need for a physical wall. In its place will be a spiritual barrier, an incredible wall of blazing fire. But God will not merely provide this fiery fume. Instead, he himself will be this supernatural wall of flames.

No enemy—physical or spiritual—can pass through God's holy wall of fire. He will protect us. He will keep us secure. We'll have nothing to fear—provided we stay inside. If we're within the Lord's city, his hedge of fire will surround us. God, through his blazing defensive shield, will envelop us with his protection.

But there's more to God's fiery fortification.

Remember, God will become this wall of fire. Fire gives off light. God's glory from his ring of fire will illuminate the city and fill it. His glory will surround all who live there.

Though Zechariah's vision looks toward our future, we can be sure God will protect us today. Let us bask in the glory of his presence.

Do we think God will become a wall of fire around us? Will we let his glory envelop us?

[Discover more about God's protection in Job 1:10. Read about his glory in Revelation 21:23.]

DAY 31: IF-THEN
ZECHARIAH 3–4

"If you will walk in obedience to me and keep my requirements, then you will govern my house and have charge of my courts, and I will give you a place among these standing here."

Zechariah 3:7

The Bible contains several thousand promises.

Some of God's promises are for specific groups of people, such as nations. Others relate to families, and many are to individuals. Then there is the timeframe to consider. Some of

God's pledges are open-ended, applying forever, whereas other ones carry a time restriction. But the best promises are the general ones made to all people throughout all time. That's because they apply to us today too.

Another consideration about God's promises is that some are unconditional, and others are conditional. Unconditional promises happen regardless. The recipient doesn't need to do anything to receive or keep what God offers.

For example, God vows to love us. This is unconditional. We don't need to do anything to earn it, and we can't do anything to lose it. God says he loves us. There are no strings attached, no fine print, and no wiggle room for him to get out of it. We can count on it because God said so.

Then there are conditional offers. God attaches stipulations. This isn't in a sleazy, trying-to-trick-you way. Instead it's in a responsible, this-is-only-fair manner. Sometimes these requirements contain prerequisites to receiving God's provision, while other times he gives conditions to retain what he offers.

Let's look at today's verse. It contains a conditional promise to one person, the high priest Joshua.

Like many conditional promises, this takes the form of if-then.

Through Zechariah, God says to the high priest Joshua that *if* you obey me and do what I say, *then* I will bless you. Specifically, God pledges to put him in charge and make him part of the leadership team.

This pledge applies specifically to Joshua. It would be wrong for us to claim this as a blanket promise that applies to us today. Consider it. Just because we obey what God tells us to do in the Bible doesn't mean he'll elevate us to a position of leadership. It may happen. Or it may not.

However, in a general sense, we see many cases when God promises various blessings to people or people groups if they obey and follow him. Therefore, we're not taking this verse out of context if we assume our obedience will lead to positive outcomes. But even if it doesn't, we should still obey God and do what he tells us to do through his instructions in the Bible and from the Holy Spirit.

How open are we to obey God's instructions? Do we have any expectations for our obedience?

[Discover more about God's unconditional love in Romans 5:5, Galatians 2:20, 1 John 4:7–8, and 1 John 4:16.]

DAY 32: DILIGENTLY OBEY
ZECHARIAH 5–6

"Those who are far away will come and help to build the temple of the Lord, and you will know that the Lord Almighty has sent me to you. This will happen if you diligently obey the Lord your God."

Zechariah 6:15

In today's verse, God gives another promise. If we consider just the first sentence of this pledge—that people will come to help rebuild the temple—it reads as unconditional, but we can't stop there. We must read the second sentence, which attaches a condition—diligent obedience—to the promise. God pledges to do something if the people do something first. They must do their part. Then he will do his.

What are they to do?

They must obey God. But more than that, they must pursue obedience with great diligence. Not partial obedience, not half-hearted obedience, and not let's-look-for-loopholes obedience. God expects a full-on, unwavering, meticulous compliance to what he says. And this isn't a go-through-the-motions conformity. Instead, God wants thorough, conscientious adherence to what he says. He wants obedience that springs from their hearts.

The Bible records many times when God tells his people to follow his instructions. Sometimes this is part of a conditional promise, but in many instances, it's simply his expectation of right behavior from his people.

But this is the only verse in the Bible where the Lord tells his people to *diligently* obey him. They must take obedience seriously.

If they do obey him diligently, what does God promise in return? It's that other people (individuals and nations) will come and help them rebuild their temple. And when this happens, it will prove the validity of Zechariah as God's spokesman.

At the time of this prophecy, the temple (and all

Jerusalem with it) is in shambles, razed by King Nebuchadnezzar several decades earlier. Though the people long to rebuild the temple, there's no realistic way they can do it. And the thought of other people—non-Jews—helping in its reconstruction is even more far-fetched.

Yet not long after Zechariah's prophecy, the temple is indeed rebuilt. It's instigated by a non-Jew, Cyrus the king of Persia. He issues a royal decree to make it happen. Not only that, but he gives back to the Jews many of the items King Nebuchadnezzar seized from the temple before he destroyed it. And Cyrus even provides the funds to pay for everything.

This near-term fulfillment of Zechariah's prophecy confirms that God spoke through him. It also implies that the people diligently obeyed God before receiving his promised restoration of the temple.

What might God do for us if we diligently obey him? Are we willing to diligently obey even if we receive no reward?

[Discover more about others helping rebuild the temple in Ezra 1:2–8, Ezra 3:7, and Ezra 6:3–12.]

DAY 33: BETTER THAN FASTING
ZECHARIAH 7–8

"Administer true justice; show mercy and compassion to one another. Do not oppress the widow or the fatherless, the foreigner or the poor. Do not plot evil against each other."

Zechariah 7:9–10

Zechariah asks the people a few pointed questions about fasting. Are they fasting for the right reasons or only going through the motions? And when they aren't fasting, and perhaps in how they end their fasts, are they honoring God or satisfying themselves?

Aside from physical health benefits, when to fast, why to fast, and how often to fast remains a spiritual mystery to me. Sometimes I fast with the right perspective, and other times I don't do so well.

Zechariah might have this struggle in mind when he cites God asking, "Was it really for me that you fasted?" Yes, we can fast for God, or we can fast for ourselves. The first brings glory to God, and the second detracts from him. If we're going to fast—or engage in any spiritual discipline—we need to do so for the right reasons. If we fast, may we do so appropriately.

But there's more.

A few verses later, Zechariah implies an alternative to fasting. Again quoting God, he tells us two things to do and two things to avoid. Following these instructions may honor God more than fasting.

First, God says he wants us to dispense genuine justice. This means to govern with integrity and not take further advantage of those already harassed.

Next, God wants us to be merciful and compassionate toward others. Offering mercy means not demanding what we're entitled to and not punishing others even if they deserve it. Mercy means to give struggling people a break. Compassion means showing empathy and taking time to understand their situations.

Beyond that, God tells us not to take advantage of widows, orphans, foreigners, or the poor. The Bible reveals God's heart for these groups of people, often telling his followers to help them and to not neglect them.

The fourth element is not to conspire to harm others. This might be out of greed, for revenge, or to be mean. Regardless, God tells us to stop hurting others.

When done right, fasting honors God. However, acting with justice, mercy, and compassion honors God *and* benefits others. So does not oppressing people or plotting evil against them.

While fasting is good, these other things may be better.

Do we, or should we, fast? Do we fast for the right reasons? Is there a better alternative?

[Discover more about what God wants from his people—and us—in Zechariah 8:16–17.]

DAY 34: PROPHECY FULFILLED
ZECHARIAH 9–10

See, your king comes to you, righteous and victorious, lowly and riding on a donkey, on a colt, the foal of a donkey.

Zechariah 9:9

Babylon has conquered God's chosen people, deporting many of them. Those who remain in Jerusalem and throughout what's left of the nation of Judah struggle to eke out their survival. They're broken, abased, and vulnerable. They so need the Savior—whom the prophets foretold—to rescue them. So when Zechariah prophesies their King coming to them, they see this as reinforcing past prophecies. Their Savior will emerge as an answer to their prayers and the fulfill-ment of many predictions.

But their King doesn't come charging in on a stallion, armed for battle, and leading a mighty military force. He comes in humility, riding a donkey. This is a sign of peace. He comes in peace, and he will promote peace.

Though the people long for a physical savior, God will send them a spiritual Savior—which is far better.

Let's fast-forward to the New Testament and read about the fulfillment of Zechariah's prophecy. Matthew, Mark, and John all record this event in their biographies of Jesus. It happens on what we call Palm Sunday, a few days before Jesus's execu-tion (Good Friday) and subsequent resurrection (Easter).

Here's what happens. As Jesus and his team walk toward Jerusalem, he sends two from his group to go on ahead to the village and look for a colt. They'll find the animal tied there, one that no one has ever ridden. They're to unfasten him and bring him to Jesus. If anyone asks what they're doing, they are to say, "The Lord needs to borrow him and will return him in a bit."

The pair do as Jesus instructed. And just as he

said, they find the colt. When they untie him, some people question them, assuming they're thieves. But once the two disciples give Jesus's answer, the people let them go.

The pair bring the colt to Jesus and throw their coats onto the animal's back to provide a makeshift saddle. Jesus mounts the colt—remember, no one's ever ridden him before, so the animal's nature is to fight anyone who climbs on his back, but this doesn't happen. Jesus rides the animal into Jerusalem. And as he does, the people line the path, spreading their coats and palm branches out before him. They shout their praise to the Lord, acknowledging Jesus as their King. Lest we have any doubt, Matthew and John both note that this fulfills Zechariah's prediction.

This is just one of the awesome ways that Jesus accomplishes Old Testament prophecy.

Do we celebrate Jesus the way the people did on the first Palm Sunday? Are we in awe of how he fulfills what the prophets foretold?

[Discover more about the fulfillment of Zechariah's prophecy in Matthew 21:1–11, Mark 11:1–11, and John 12:12–19.]

DAY 35: SHEPHERDS AND SHEEP
ZECHARIAH 11–12

*The flock detested me, and I grew weary of them and said,
"I will not be your shepherd."*

Zechariah 11:8–9

As Zechariah wraps up his book, he makes some perplexing references to shepherds and their sheep, about bad shepherds and bad flocks. These allusions apply to Zechariah's audience, look prophetically into the future, and provide a valuable illustration for us today.

This passage is about God and his people, about leaders and their charges, and it's about us. But each emerges with a bit of perplexing confusion. Zechariah seems to be talking figuratively while at the same time personifying God.

Zechariah writes, "The flock hates me. I'm sick and tired of them. I'm done with them. Let them die."

If we consider God as our Shepherd and we as his sheep, I wonder if we sometimes hate him the way these sheep hate their shepherd. Or at least, how often do we act like we hate him? I get that.

What horrifies me, however, is the thought of God giving up on us and walking away, like Zechariah wants to give up on his sheep and abandon them. Yet it's exactly what God does in this text with his chosen people. May we never hate God. More important, may God never give up on us.

Now let's apply this to today's congregations and their leaders.

Most church members at most churches adore, or at least respect, their leaders, who are their preachers, or more biblically, their shepherds. Yet I've seen instances where things go awry, where the church flock—the sheep—despise their leader, their shepherd. Though this is sometimes the fault of the leader, more often, it's the result of bad sheep who misbehave, want their own way, and don't follow well.

Other times I've seen shepherds who've given up on their flocks. These ministers face burn out, exhaustion, and function in survival mode. This may be due to their own issues, but I suspect that in many cases it's a human reaction to how the flocks treat them.

Sometimes churches who disrespect their pastors and the pastors who've given up on their churches deserve each other. The blame lies with both parties. Unfortunately, once a church finds itself in this situation, without God's supernatural intervention, a broken shepherd-flock relationship is hard to fix.

God gives us shepherds to lead, protect, and nurture us. But we need to be good sheep too. We need to speak well of our shepherds, stand up for them, and respect them. If we can't do that, we're hurting our shepherds and damaging the rest of the flock. If we aren't careful, we'll be the cause for the exact malady Zechariah writes about in today's text.

With God's help, may we strive to be good sheep. May we pray for our shepherds to lead us well.

Are we good sheep? Do we respect and follow our shepherds?

[Discover more about what Jesus says about shepherds in Matthew 9:36, John 10:1–3, and John 10:11–18, as well as Zechariah 13:7, which Jesus quotes in Matthew 26:31 and Mark 14:27.]

DIG DEEPER: THIRTY PIECES OF SILVER

So they paid me thirty pieces of silver. And the Lord said to me, "Throw it to the potter" . . . So I took the thirty pieces of silver and threw them to the potter at the house of the Lord.

Zechariah 11:12–13

S tuffed in the middle of Zechariah's message about shepherds and their flocks, we learn of him receiving a payment of thirty pieces of silver. He throws the money at the potter. It's a weird thing that God tells Zechariah to do. But the prophet obeys.

This surely perplexes the people of Zechariah's day, but with a little thought, it makes sense to us now. Do thirty pieces of silver sound familiar? For payment of thirty silver coins, Judas sells out Jesus, handing him over to the Jewish religious leaders.

I'm not sure what Judas was thinking, or it could be he wasn't thinking of anything but the money. But when Judas sees that Jesus will die because of his selfish betrayal of the Lord, guilt overcomes him. He confesses his sin and tries to return the money. When the corrupt religious leaders won't take back the silver, Judas throws the money at them and storms off. He kills himself out of remorse.

The religious leaders can't receive the silver as an offering. They call it blood money, even though they initiated the unlawful payment. So they take the money, buy a field from a potter, and use it as a cemetery for foreigners.

Interestingly, Matthew credits this prophecy to Jeremiah instead of Zechariah. The verses in Jeremiah that Bible scholars point to don't make as strong of a connection as what Zechariah wrote. Though we don't know why Matthew wrote *Jeremiah*, instead of *Jeremiah and Zechariah*, or just *Zechariah*, let's not lose the main point that the Old Testament prophets foretold what Judas would do.

Though we would shudder at the idea of betraying Jesus, how might we have turned on him in other ways?

[Discover more about the fulfillment of this prophecy in Matthew 27:3–10, as well as Acts 1:18–19. Read what Jeremiah has to say about a potter and silver in Jeremiah 19:1–13 and Jeremiah 32:6–9.]

DAY 36: OUR PRESENT AND FUTURE HOPE

ZECHARIAH 13–14

"They will call on my name and I will answer them; I will say, 'They are my people,' and they will say, 'The Lord is our God.'"

Zechariah 13:9

After Zechariah's discouraging implication that God is weary of his people and will no longer be their Shepherd, Zechariah has some good news. He concludes his prophetic writings with an optimistic prophecy of a better tomorrow. This is a hope that the people of his day can anticipate. But it's also a hope we can claim today.

What is this grand, future expectation?

For the people of Zechariah's day, when they pray to God, he will again answer. They can count on him to be there for them. He will again call them his people, and they will again call him their Lord. They will turn to each other. Reunited.

This union with God reminds us of how Adam and Eve walked in the garden of Eden with their Creator. In the cool of the evening, they hung out and enjoyed one another's company. They lived in community with God in his creation, spending time with one another.

We can also anticipate community with our Creator today. Though we don't physically walk with him in a garden each evening, when we call out to him, he answers. He is our Lord, and we are his people.

But Zechariah has more. This message for the people's future is for our future too. We await it in eager expectation . . . but for what?

Centuries after Zechariah, the disciple John has a compelling vision of the future, a look into *our* future. In his forward-looking revelation, John writes of a time when all nations and all kings will come together in the holy temple of the Lord and the Lamb. What a day that will be, a day we hope for and long to see.

We can look forward to this time with great anticipation, the day when God will reign as King over the whole earth. He will become the Lord of everyone. His name will stand as the only name for people to call on for their rescue, for their salvation.

This will restore our community with God, just as he intended from the beginning.

Where do we place our hope? Do we live lives that reflect both our present hope and our future hope?

[Discover more about our future hope in Zechariah 14:9 and Revelation 21:22–26.]

JOEL

The Bible tells us nothing about Joel other than that his father is Pethuel. From Scripture, it's not possible to place him chronologically, but many Bible scholars view him as a contemporary of Malachi, possibly with overlapping ministries. Joel's prophecies talk more about locusts—which represent widespread destruction—than any other prophet.

Here is an overview of Joel:

Known As: Joel son of Pethuel

Addresses: the exiles who have returned to Judah from Babylon

Contemporaries: Malachi

New Testament Mentions: Acts 2:16

New Testament Quotations:

- Joel 2:28–32 in Acts 2:16–21
- Joel 2:32 in Romans 10:13

Homonymous Mentions: Fourteen other men in the Bible have the same name, but the prophet Joel is the most notable.

DAY 37: A HOLY FAST
JOEL 1

Declare a holy fast; call a sacred assembly. Summon the elders and all who live in the land to the house of the Lord your God, and cry out to the Lord.

Joel 1:14

A curious phrase pops up in the book of Joel: a holy fast. Joel uses this phrase twice, but no other biblical writer does. What does he mean by it?

If a fast can be holy, consider the opposite. Can a fast be unholy? I suspect so. An unholy fast might be fasting for the wrong reasons, under incorrect expectations, or with a misguided focus. As a result, it's not a holy act, but the opposite, an unholy one.

A spiritual fast is going without something, such as food, to draw closer to God. By implication, fasting should emerge as a holy act. So why does the prophet Joel need to specify a holy fast?

It's to make the point that the people's fasts aren't holy. This might be because they've lost sight of why they were fasting. It could be they're going through the motions of forgoing food but have forgotten about God, who should be their fasting focus.

When done for the right reasons, a fast is a physical denial that elevates our spiritual awareness. When done for the wrong reasons, a fast is a physical denial that makes us feel deprived, without providing spiritual benefits. In doing so, we forgo any divine results. That would make it an unholy fast: secular and spiritually meaningless.

Fasting for health reasons is fine, but if you practice the spiritual discipline of fasting, examine your motives. Consider the outcomes. If a fast falls short of what it once was or what it could be, consider the possibility that it has become an unholy fast. We should seek God to reorient our perspectives and attitudes so that we can experience the holiness of fasting.

And if we don't fast, should we consider doing so?

Though I'm not aware of the Bible ever commanding us to fast, people in both the Old and New Testaments—including Jesus—follow this practice. If God is calling you to fast, seek to do so for the right reasons: to focus on him and draw closer.

When we fast, is it a holy fast? How can we keep the focus of our fasting on God?

[Discover more about fasting in Jeremiah 14:12 and Joel 2:15.]

DAY 38: SWARMS OF LOCUSTS
JOEL 2–3

"I will repay you for the years the locusts have eaten."

Joel 2:25

Classified as one of the Bible's prophetic books, the book of Joel contains a foretelling of the future. But this short, three-chapter book emerges more as poetry than prophecy, revealing multiple levels of meaning for us to discover.

The name of the book is the same as the prophet who receives God's oracle—Joel. The nemesis of Joel's story is a horde of locusts.

The most significant mention of locusts in the

Bible is one of the plagues that befell Egypt in Moses's day. To get the Pharaoh's attention and bring about the release of God's people, God told Moses to extend his hand over all Egypt. When Moses did, God whipped up a strong wind that blew in hordes of locusts to swarm across the land. They devoured everything in sight, everything that was still growing in the fields after the prior plague of hail had destroyed most of it. Because of the locusts, all plant life was gone.

Another biblical mention of locusts is the unique diet of John the Baptist: locusts and wild honey. But aside from the life-giving nourishment the locusts provide to John, all the other biblical references to locusts relate to plague, destruction, and death—be it literal or figurative.

Joel's message follows the ravaging nature of locusts but to an even greater extent. It's one of unprecedented destruction. This mass of locusts will eat everything in sight, devastating all plants, stripping them of all foliage. In the process, the locusts remove the sustenance that the plants produce. Having no crops to eat, both people and animals will suffer.

God will send these locusts to get the people's attention. Nothing like this has ever happened in their memory. An army of locusts, invading their land like another nation, stripping it bare. God wants the people to return to him. Sound familiar? He wants them to return to him in wholehearted-ness, with fasting, and in remorse.

Yet after the locusts cause their destruction, God promises that a grand and glorious redemption will follow. He pledges to restore the years of produce and prosperity that the locusts ate.

What have swarms of locusts stripped from us? How should we react?

[Discover more about locusts in Exodus 10:1–20, Deuteronomy 28:38, Joel 1:4, Matthew 3:4, and Mark 1:6.]

MALACHI

The name Malachi occurs only once in the Bible. The reference gives no background information about him. Bible scholars believe he is a contemporary of Joel. Malachi addresses many of the ways that God's people fall short of his expectations.

Here is an overview of Malachi:

Addresses: the exiles who have returned to Judah from Babylon

Contemporaries: Joel

New Testament Mentions: none

New Testament Quotations:

- Malachi 1:2–3 in Romans 9:13
- Malachi 3:1 in Matthew 11:10, Mark 1:2, and Luke 7:27

Homonymous Mentions: There are no other men in the Bible named Malachi.

DAY 39: CLOSE CHURCH?
MALACHI 1–2

"Oh, that one of you would shut the temple doors, so that you would not light useless fires on my altar! I am not pleased with you," says the Lord Almighty, "and I will accept no offering from your hands."

Malachi 1:10

In the book of Malachi, God laments over his people. At one point he criticizes the priests because they show contempt for him. The people's worship is so off track that God wishes one of the priests would just shut the temple doors. This would at least keep them from lighting useless fires on his altar, from presenting him with ineffective worship. He's so frustrated with them that he won't accept their offerings.

So why bother? Just close the temple. This is a shocking thought, a seemingly heretical idea.

Yet we hear of church closings all the time. It's usually due to one of two things. Often it's for a lack of funds—because the people left aren't giving enough to keep the church doors open.

The other reason churches close is a lack of people. These two reasons often interconnect. Attendance drops. Giving decreases. They cut programs. Attendance drops more. A downward spiral continues. Eventually, there aren't enough people left to do the work and not enough money to pay the bills. Closing is the only option.

But I've never heard of a church closing because their worship of God has become offensive to him. Yet I wonder if this spiritual malady isn't more common than we realize. Does God grow sick of these misled congregations and wish they would just close? These spiritually impotent churches are even worse off than the ones that no longer have enough people or money to continue.

Most churches become institutions over time. As institutions, they seek to perpetuate themselves regardless of the circumstances. In their struggle for survival, they lose sight of why they existed in the first place. Instead of seeking to serve their communities and offer salvation through Jesus, their focus turns inward. Their priority becomes self-preservation.

Some would argue that God's words through his prophet Malachi apply only to the priests and the temple of his day. Projecting them onto today's church is taking the text out of context. Perhaps. But if we can't learn insights from the Old Testament, why bother to read it?

Should we interpret Malachi's words to shut the doors of the temple as a warning to take seriously today? When our churches and services become spiritually dead, God may want us to close our doors and not further profane his reputation.

Are our churches at risk of becoming spiritually dead? Are we?

[Discover more about being spiritually dead in Ephesians 2:1–9, Colossians 2:13, and Jude 1:12.]

DIG DEEPER: Q & A WITH GOD

"I have loved you," says the Lord. "But you ask, 'How have you loved us?'"

Malachi 1:2

I n the short book of Malachi, we find a recurring phrase: *but you ask* (along with a few variations thereof). This turns into a question-and-answer monologue, with God voicing the people's unspoken questions and him answering.

Malachi records the whole thing. Although Malachi lives in a culture vastly different from ours, these are lessons we can learn—if we're willing to listen.

Question: How have you loved us?

Answer: Consider your ancestors Jacob and Esau. I loved Jacob and hated Esau. Consider how I treated Esau (Malachi 1:2–3).

Question: How have we shown contempt for your name?

Answer: By presenting me with defiled offerings (Malachi 1:6–7).

Question: How have we defiled you?

Answer: By giving me what is not good enough for anyone else (Malachi 1:7–8).

Question: Why do you no longer pay attention to our offerings or accept them?

Answer: You have been unfaithful to your wife and broken your marriage vows (Malachi 2:13–14). Consider this on both a physical and spiritual level.

Question: How have we wearied you?

Answer: By doing bad, yet claiming it is good and that it somehow pleases me (Malachi 2:17).

Question: How are we to return to you?

Answer: Stop robbing me (Malachi 3:7–8).

Question: How do we rob you?

Answer: By withholding some of your tithes and offerings (Malachi 3:8–10).

Question: What have we said against you?

Answer: Saying it's futile to serve me when I don't bless you for doing what I expect (Malachi 3:13–14).

What questions do we have for God? More important, what questions might God have for us?

[Discover more about some questions Abraham asks God in Genesis 18:23–32.]

DAY 40: GOD CHALLENGES US TO TEST HIM

MALACHI 3–4

"Test me in this," says the Lord Almighty, "and see if I will not throw open the floodgates of heaven and pour out so much blessing that there will not be room enough to store it."

Malachi 3:10

Through Malachi, God reminds the people that he does not change. But the people have. They've ignored his commands and turned away from him. He calls them to turn back to him. And if they do, he will return to them. This is another one of God's conditional promises.

But the people play dumb. They pretend they don't know what he's talking about, that they don't understand how they can return to him.

God gets right to the point. "Stop robbing me." By not robbing him, they will implicitly return to him.

They continue to pretend they don't understand. "How in the world are we stealing from you?"

They're robbing him through their tithes and offerings.

Malachi doesn't identify exactly how this theft occurs. It might be that they give God nothing. Or it could be that they give him only part of what they're supposed to. Another consideration is that instead of giving him the best, their "first fruits," they give him the leftovers no one wants. They offer him what is worthless to them.

Regardless of their shortfalls, God feels cheated. Robbed.

Because they have denied him what he is due, the whole nation has fallen under a curse: a lack of prosperity, poverty.

God challenges the people to put him to a test. They are to stop stealing from him and fully give to him what he has requested. He wants them to offer what he is due, the things he has commanded.

When they do this, he will pour out his blessings on them. The floodgates will open, and they'll have more than they need. Their poverty will end. Prosperity will begin.

Some people say, "You can't outgive God." It's true that God has unlimited resources while ours have limits. In truth, he has much more to give us than we can ever hope to give him.

To the people of Malachi's day, God says that they are to test him in this. Should we do the same now? Of course, if we give to God merely because of what we hope he will give back to us, our motives are wrong, and we should expect nothing.

Why do we give to God? What is our attitude with the things we offer to him?

[Discover more about giving in Proverbs 11:24, Matthew 22:21, and Luke 6:29. Read about what God desires in Hosea 6:6, Matthew 9:13, and Matthew 12:7.]

If you liked *Minor Prophets Bible Study,* please leave a review online. Your review will help others discover this book and encourage them to read it too.

Thank you.

THE 40-DAY BIBLE STUDY SERIES

Which book do you want to read next in the 40-Day Bible Study Series?

- Dear Theophilus (the Gospel of Luke, formerly That You May Know)
- Acts Bible Study (formerly Tongues of Fire)
- Isaiah Bible Study (formerly For Unto Us)
- Dear Theophilus, Job (formerly I Hope in Him)
- Living Water (John)
- Love Is Patient (1 and 2 Corinthians)
- Revelation Bible Study
- Love One Another (1, 2, and 3 John)

- Run with Perseverance (Hebrews)
- James and Jude Bible Study
- Matthew Bible Study
- 1 & 2 Peter Bible Study
- Mark Bible Study

FOR SMALL GROUPS, SUNDAY SCHOOL, AND CLASSES

Minor Prophets Bible Study makes an ideal eight-week Bible study discussion guide for small groups, Sunday School, and classes. To prepare for the conversation, read one chapter of this book each weekday, Monday through Friday.

- Week 1: read 1 through 5.
- Week 2: read 6 through 10.
- Week 3: read 11 through 15.
- Week 4: read 16 through 20.
- Week 5: read 21 through 25.
- Week 6: read 26 through 30.
- Week 7: read 31 through 35.
- Week 8: read 36 through 40.

When you get together, discuss the questions at the end of each chapter. The leader can use all the questions to guide this discussion or pick which ones to focus on.

Before beginning the discussion, pray as a group. Ask for Holy Spirit insight and clarity.

As you consider each chapter's questions:

- Look for how this can grow your understanding of the Bible.
- Evaluate how this can expand your faith perspective.
- Consider what you need to change in how you live your lives.

End by asking God to help apply what you've learned.

May God bless you as you read and study his Word.

IF YOU'RE NEW TO THE BIBLE

Each entry in this book contains Bible references. These can guide you if you want to learn more. If you're not familiar with the Bible, here's an overview to get you started, give some context, and minimize confusion.

First, the Bible is a collection of works written by various authors over several centuries. Think of the Bible as a diverse anthology of godly communication. It contains historical accounts, poetry, songs, letters of instruction and encouragement, messages from God sent through his representatives, and prophecies.

Most versions of the Bible have sixty-six books grouped into two sections: The Old Testament and the New Testament. The Old Testament contains thirty-nine books that precede and anticipate Jesus. The New Testament includes twenty-seven books and covers Jesus's life and the work of his followers.

The reference notations in the Bible, such as Romans 3:23, are analogous to line numbers in a Shakespearean play. They serve as a study aid. Since the Bible is much longer and more complex than a play, its reference notations are more involved.

As already mentioned, the Bible is an amalgam of books, or sections, such as Genesis, Matthew, or Acts. These are the names given to them, over time, based on the piece's author, audience, or purpose.

In the 1200s, each book was divided into chapters, such as Acts 2 or Psalm 23. In the 1500s, the chapters were further subdivided into verses, such as John 3:16. Let's use this as an example.

The name of the book (John) appears first, followed by the chapter number (3), a colon, and then the verse number (16). Sometimes called a chapter-verse reference notation, this helps people quickly find a specific text regardless of their version of the Bible.

Although the goal was to place these chapter and verse divisions at logical breaks, they sometimes seem arbitrary. Therefore, it's good practice to read what precedes and follows each passage you're studying. The text before or after it may contain relevant insights into the portion you're exploring.

Here's how to look up a specific passage in the Bible based on its reference: Most Bibles contain a table of contents, which gives the page number for the beginning of each book. Start there. Locate the book you want to read, and turn to that page. Then flip forward to the chapter you want. Last, skim that chapter to locate the specific verse.

If you want to read online, enter the reference into BibleGateway.com or BibleHub.com. Also check out the YouVersion app.

Learn more about the greatest book ever written at ABibleADay.com, which provides a Bible blog, summaries of the books of the Bible, a dictionary of Bible terms, Bible reading plans, and other resources.

ABOUT PETER DEHAAN

Peter DeHaan, PhD, wants to change the world one word at a time. His books and blog posts discuss God, the Bible, and church, geared toward spiritual seekers and church dropouts. Many people feel church has let them down, and Peter seeks to encourage them as they search for a place to belong.

But he's not afraid to ask tough questions or make religious people squirm. He's not trying to be provocative. Instead, he seeks truth, even if it makes people uncomfortable. Peter urges Christians to push past the status quo and reexamine how they practice their faith in every part of their lives.

Peter earned his doctorate, awarded with high distinction, from Trinity College of the Bible and Theological Seminary. He lives with his wife in beautiful Southwest Michigan and wrangles crossword puzzles in his spare time.

A lifelong student of Scripture, Peter wrote the 1,000-page website ABibleADay.com to encourage people to explore the Bible, the greatest book ever written. His popular blog addresses biblical Christianity to build a faith that matters.

Read his blog, receive his newsletter, and learn more at PeterDeHaan.com.

BOOKS BY PETER DEHAAN

40-Day Bible Study Series

Dear Theophilus (the Gospel of Luke)

Acts Bible Study

Isaiah Bible Study

Job Bible Study

Living Water (John)

Love Is Patient (1 and 2 Corinthians)

Revelation Bible Study

Love One Another (1, 2, and 3 John)

Run with Perseverance (Hebrews)

James and Jude Bible Study

Matthew Bible Study

1 & 2 Peter Bible Study

Mark Bible Study

Holiday Celebration Devotionals

The Advent of Jesus

The Passion of Jesus (Lent)

The Victory of Jesus (Easter)

The Ministry of Jesus

Thanksgiving with Jesus

Bible Character Sketches Series

Women of the Bible

The Friends and Foes of Jesus

Old Testament Sinners and Saints

More Old Testament Sinners and Saints

Heroes and Heavies of the Apocrypha

200 Old Testament Sinners and Saints

Visiting Churches Series

52 Churches

The 52 Churches Workbook

More Than 52 Churches

The More Than 52 Churches Workbook

Visiting Online Church

Shopping for Church

Other Books

Elephant God

Jesus's Broken Church

Martin Luther's 95 Theses (formerly *95 Tweets*)

The Christian Church's LGBTQ Failure

Bridging the Sacred-Secular Divide (formerly *Woodpecker Wars*)

Beyond Psalm 150

How Big Is Your Tent?

For the latest list of all Peter's books, go to PeterDeHaan.com/books.